D1133232

WHAT IS MODERNISM?

WHAT IS MODERNISM?

BY

LEIGHTON PARKS, D.D.

RECTOR OF ST. BARTHOLOMEW'S CHURCH IN THE CITY OF NEW YORK
AUTHOR OF "THE CRISIS OF THE CHURCHES," "ENGLISH
WAYS AND BY WAYS," ETC., ETC.

"*Every scribe which is instructed unto the kingdom of heaven is like unto a man that is an householder, which bringeth forth out of his treasure things new and old.*"

ST. MATTHEW

CHARLES SCRIBNER'S SONS

NEW YORK · LONDON

1924

Printed in the United States of America

Published March, 1924

TO

THE MEMORY OF

THE REVEREND CYRIL W. EMMET

DEAN OF UNIVERSITY COLLEGE, OXFORD

SCHOLAR, PREACHER, SAINT

WHO DIED WHILE PREACHING IN ST. BARTHOLOMEW'S CHURCH

"THE SIGNIFICANCE OF CHRIST IN MODERN LIFE"

THIS BOOK IS REVERENTLY DEDICATED

PREFACE

When I was asked by some of my friends to write a short book which should explain to people who were not versed in theology or ecclesiastical history what the present controversy which is disturbing all the churches really means, I hesitated to undertake the task. In the first place, I felt that my present duties required all my time and energy, and that to undertake any new work might lead to neglect of the one for which I am primarily responsible. But even if I had the leisure, I questioned if one who can lay no claim to technical scholarship was fitted to write such a book as they had in mind. The reader may then ask why I should now have undertaken that which I once felt I ought not to undertake. The answer is that, first, my friends felt that the lack of technical scholarship might not be altogether a disadvantage; that what is needed is not a book which those who are more or less familiar with critical problems would care to read—there is no lack of such books—but one which the "wayfaring man," the plain people, would find helpful, and that such a book might well be written by a plain man. This judgment was confirmed by an experience to which I hope I may be allowed to refer.

When the controversy which had been confined to other churches was suddenly brought into the life of the Episcopal Church, I felt called upon to utter a protest, which was given wide publicity by the newspapers, not only of this country but of Europe as well. The result of that unsought notoriety brought to me hundreds of letters, from almost every State in the Union, from Canada as far west as Vancouver, a few from England, and one from Australia. These letters were a revelation of the confusion and panic, the deep distress and the longing for a freedom of faith which would enable men and women no longer satisfied with the old expressions of faith to worship God in spirit and in truth.

Some of these letters were brutally abusive and frankly stated that no fate—here or hereafter—was too dreadful for the man who would disturb the peace of the Church. But the instinctive reaction of resentment was restrained by the thought that these men and women are frightened and therefore are not entirely responsible. They are in the state of mind of those religious people of whom Jesus spoke when he told his disciples that the religious people of his day would desire to put them out of the synagogue—yea, put them to death, because they thought that in this way they would be doing God's service. They are like the poor peasant woman who, when John Huss was bound to the stake to be burned, brought a little bundle of faggots and cast them on the pile that the fire might burn more fiercely; but the martyr understood that she was not doing this because she was a wicked woman but because she was frightened. She really believed that he was the enemy of God and of His Church, so he murmured "*sancta simplicitas*"—holy simplicity. So I think we should say of the religious men and women who to-day are in a panic.

There were other letters which disagreed and said so, giving reasons which deserve respectful consideration.

Many were from clergymen of whom I have

never heard and who had never heard of me before, who were comforted and cheered to find that one, whose only claim to speak with authority was due to long service in the ministry of the Church, felt at liberty to say things which they had felt but had supposed no one else in good standing in the Church would say. Like the prophet of old, they supposed that "they only were left." To quote but one of these letters: "One of the most important results [of the protest] has been that hundreds of young men who are being driven from a contemplated life in the ministry of Christ's Gospel, by the rigidity of the demands upon their credulity, will be given sufficient liberty of thought to make them feel comfortable in the work God really intended them to do."

From professors in colleges, from physicians and students of science, from lawyers and men and women of high intelligence, came letters which might have led me to think of myself more highly than I ought to think, had it not been that I was saddened and sobered by letters from devout people who were in trouble and perplexity. Some wrote that they had not been to the Holy Communion for years because they had been led to believe that no one was welcome there save those only who could give assent to every article of the Creed in its literal sense; but "if we have the liberty which you claim, we are going to Communion on Christmas Day."

But the saddest were from those good and devout people who said that they had been brought up to believe the traditional theology—they had never given it much thought but simply accepted it—but whose children were now asking questions which they could not answer. "What are we to say to them? Can you tell us of some one book, not too long or technical or expensive, which we can read so as to understand better what the whole controversy is about." This I interpreted as a call from the "lost sheep in the wilderness" and therefore, while I hope I have not left my own flock, I have found time, somehow, to put down on paper what I hope may be found helpful by way of explanation. No short book can answer offhand any question that may be asked, and it may be that some will feel that this book is more technical than they had desired. But I think there is nothing in it which a man or woman unfamiliar with theological or ecclesiastical history will not understand, if they will give to it the serious thought which the subject demands. It may serve as an introduction to more serious study, and, therefore, I have added at the end of the volume a list of books which the reader may desire to consult; and the numbers which follow certain paragraphs refer to these books.

"Modernism" is the name which has been given to the movement which is supposed to be the cause of the present distress. But it is not modern. It is as old as religion itself. But those who are not familiar with the history of religious thought not unnaturally suppose that it is some new thing. For that very reason it attracts the curious who have no deep spiritual soil and repels those who are suspicious of anything that has not the stamp of antiquity. It is new in this sense: that the questions which it has been compelled to discuss have not been before the public in the form in which they now appear. It is not Modernism which has caused the unrest; it is the great tidal wave following the earthquake of the war which has submerged many things which had previously been supposed to be fundamental. This is true in every department of life. International relations, the demands of patriotism, political and economic "foundations" have been shaken. So have social, industrial, and moral foundations.

It was inevitable that religious foundations should also be shaken. Now, just as in every other department of life, those who are seeking to find what really are the foundations—as distinguished from what had popularly been supposed to be foundations—should be thought to have no reverence for the past and to intend to destroy the "customs which have been delivered to us," so in the field of religion those men who are seeking to find what are the real foundations are supposed to be trying to destroy the foundations. These are called "Modernists." But if we were to read carefully the book in the New Testament written by a "Modernist" of the days which followed the destruction of Jerusalem—the Epistle to the Hebrews—we might find that he was not trying to destroy the foundations; he was trying to show what the foundations really were. "The things which have been shaken, have been shaken because they could not remain,"—they were not foundations at all. So the object of the shaking was to reveal the true foundations, which can never be shaken. That is the way the Modernist would describe himself.

But the vast majority of men lack the boldness of faith; they think that the cure of the present distress is to be found by a return to the past—pre-war conditions—and that if we could do that, we should have peace in every department of life. It is a natural feeling. We see that it has always been the temper of the timid in every crisis of the world. When Jerusalem fell, there were devout Jews who believed that it could be rebuilt. When the Holy Roman Empire came to an end, the Council of Vienna thought it could be re-established. The Royalists in France thought that there the Revolution was but a passing storm. There were Loyalists who still dreamed of a return to England after the battle of Bunker Hill. But those who think that the shadow can be made to return on the dial will find that the prophet's promise expresses biting irony. "Behold I make all things new," says the seer of the Apocalypse. "Are we then to look for another?" ask the troubled souls. "Has He not come?" The Modernist believes that He has come, but he also believes that He is to come again. He is looking for the "Christ that is to be" and he believes that He does not intend to restore again the kingdom of Israel but to reveal the Kingdom of God.

"But," says the Fundamentalist, "was not the Kingdom of God revealed before the war by the Church?" That is the question which the Modernist would have the Fundamentalist seriously consider. Are not many men saying —both those within as well as those without the Church—that the most awful revelation of the war was the impotence of the churches? And was not that impotence due in part to the fact that the men who were assembled to the battle showed that multitudes of them were ignorant of the first principles of the teaching of Christ? What had they been taught? Some of them had been taught the tradition of the fathers, and it was found that it did not stand the test of war and suffering and death. Have we not all known young men who went to the war in the simple faith which they had been taught, and returned in the spirit of scepticism of either the goodness or the power of God? We must get to the foundations of faith before we can discuss what are the foundations of Christian faith.

The fact is that the Modernist is the least interested in the particular questions which have been given prominence in the present controversy in the churches; the infallibility of the Bible, the authority of the Creeds, the importance of alleged "historical facts," all seem to him irrelevant to the fundamental questions which the young are asking to-day. Look at the books which are being used in our colleges today;[1] ask the men who are preaching in the universities what questions the intelligent youth are asking; look at the questions propounded in magazines, novels, and newspapers, and it will be found that the thinking men and women outside the churches—and it is a growing number—are not indifferent to religion but are indifferent to the things about which the churches seem so excited. The Modernist may be wrong in regard to every question now being discussed, and yet may be the one who understands that the fundamental questions which must be answered are: "What is God?" "How do you know there is a God?" "How do you know that religion is not an illusion?" The Modernist is convinced that no external authority can answer these questions in a way that will satisfy the deepest longings of the soul. He believes that men must be shown the eternal foundation on which the soul has always rested—the experience of the soul in touch with Reality. It is because he is interested in such questions that he deplores the confusion caused by those who would inject at such a time the discussion of questions, which, however they may be decided, will add nothing to the "assurance of faith." He would have kept silent, were it not that there is one question involved in the controversy which may lead to the driving out of the churches or the shutting of the door of the churches to men who believe that the Church is the witness to the faith—the faith which made the Bible and the Church and the Creeds. So he has been led from the essential to the unessential to defend the liberty of the Christian man. His object, then, in discussing the questions with which this book deals, is not to convince any one that he is right and some one else is wrong in regard to the particulars, but simply that it may be recognized that none of them is fundamental. If that could be recognized, there might come such a union of men of good will in all the churches as would make the Church a living power and the home of those who are deeply religious and at the same time profoundly "unorthodox."

I hold no brief for the word "Modernism." The reaction to words is a curious psychological —I suspect pathological—phenomenon. The oft-told tale of the good woman who found "Mesopotamia" a soothing word is one example. But how do those differ from her who are exasperated by the word "Modernism"? To them it connotes a seeking after new things and never coming to the truth; to be as vulgar as certain *nouveaux riches* who are ashamed of their humble origin; to smack of the Pharisaism which thanks God that it is not as unintelligent as other men are—even as this Fundamentalist. If this book succeeds in lessening that prejudice, it will have been worth writing, even if it fail to lead the reader to see that Modernism is really an intelligent, reverent attempt to bring out of the Church's treasure "things new as well as old."

I am deeply indebted to the Reverend William H. P. Hatch, D.D., of the Episcopal Theological School, Cambridge, for reading one chapter of this book and giving me the help of his exact scholarship; and to the Reverend Roland Cotton

Smith, D.D., who read the whole manuscript and made suggestions which only such a literary artist could give. I need not say that for no part of this book is either of them responsible. To my secretary, Miss Filomena Ricciardi, I am especially indebted; she has been both hands and eyes to me, and without her intelligent and willing help the book could not have been written at all.

L. P.

Festival of the Conversion of St. Paul, 1924.

CONTENTS

WHAT IS MODERNISM?

CHAPTER I

MODERNISM

I. THE ORIGIN OF THE NAME

The name "Modernism" is not one of which Protestants can be proud, for it was a term used somewhat contemptuously by Pope Pius X in the encyclical Pascendi (1907) condemning certain social, philosophical, and historical movements in the Roman Catholic Church. By "Modernism" he probably meant "new-fangled notions."[1] But it was more than that.

The movement described as "Modernism" may be said to have arisen in Italy and France after the close of the Franco-Prussian War and the unification of Italy, in an attempt by devout Catholics to adjust themselves to the new political condition. This, however, was but one of the forms the new movement was taking. The traditional philosophy, which taught that the intellect was the organ of natural knowledge and of what was called "natural" religion but that the Ultimate Reality could only be revealed by external authority, was being called in question by the new philosophy,—later to be developed among others, by Bergson and William James,—which was emphasizing the influence of the subconscious emotions actuating the will. And thirdly, the critical examination of historical documents which had led to a re-reading of secular history, was leading to a re-investigation of the origins of Christianity. Strauss' work, which turned the Gospel story into mythology, and Renan's, which wrote it as a romance, were profoundly distasteful to religious souls. Therefore, men like Duchesne and Loisy began the investigation of the origins of Christianity uninfluenced by the presuppositions of Strauss or the romantic imagination of Renan.

In spite of the protests from individual bishops and priests, Leo XIII, a great statesman, while he could have had little sympathy with the movement, at first followed the wise rule of allowing the tares to grow together with the wheat until the harvest. As a result, the Modernist "tares" grew apace and were finally condemned by him.

Among English Catholics there was no need for political activity. That they had long enjoyed. But two men became the leaders of the philosophic and critical historical movements. The first was Baron von Hügel,[2] still living, still in communion with the Church, and one of the leaders of a spiritual interpretation of the universe. The other, Father Tyrrell,[3] whose more popular writings expressed the result of critical study, was having an influence not only among the laity but among the young priests as well.

When Pius X became Pope, he decided that the "harvest" had arrived and he gathered up the tares in bundles and burned them—burned them in the only way that modern civilization permits; the priests were forbidden (in accordance with Leo XIII's encyclical) to write or speak in contradiction of the prevailing philosophy which had been formulated by St. Thomas Aquinas, and men like Loisy and Tyrrell were excommunicated. The latter died declaring himself still a faithful member of the Church, but Loisy, deprived of the companionship of his brethren, upon which a priest, separated from all family ties, is peculiarly dependent, drifted far away not only from the tradition but, as many believe, from the essentials of the Christian faith. Modernism was suppressed.

Certainly there are advantages in autocracy

and there is a tendency in all the Protestant churches to revert to the methods of autocracy. But they can hardly expect to produce the submission that follows the word of an infallible Pope. In a democracy men must be convinced of error, or, what is supposed to be their error must be acknowledged to be an aspect of truth, before there can be peace. Whether the suppression of the expression of opinion has really destroyed the root of Modernism in the Roman Catholic Church, time alone will show. There is a wide-spread suspicion that suppression has not eradicated the evil.[4]

This sketch of the rise and fall of Modernism in the Roman Catholic Church will help us to understand its nature in the Protestant Churches of America. Politically, it is interested in social reform. Philosophically, it is more interested in psychology than in metaphysics. And in its historical or critical form, it is a movement "inspired by a desire to bring the tradition of Christian belief and practice into close relation with the intellectual habits and social aspirations of our own time."[5]

But while it is called a "movement" it is not to be supposed that it is the movement of a party. It is the movement of individuals. What one of its most uncompromising critics has said is true: "If, . . . we criticise any statements of the Modernist type, it must always be distinctly understood that they are quoted as the opinions of an individual . . . and that quite likely some at least would qualify them, or reserve judgment, or repudiate what the individual author says."[6] In other words, a certain socialistic tendency in the political movement is repudiated by many Modernists, such as Dean Inge, and many who are Traditionalists in their philosophy are strongly socialistic in their political tendencies. Bishop Gore may be called a Modernist judged by his critical examination of the Old Testament, while philosophically he is a Traditionalist.

In other words, Modernism is not a body of doctrine. It is a state of mind. It is an attempt to "justify the ways of God to man," that is, to man in the twentieth century. And the problem is this: Must the men and women who are breathing the new atmosphere of freedom, of the larger knowledge which has come as the result of scientific discovery, psychological experience and historical investigation, be told that they must accept opinions which were once believed to be true or abandon the communion of the Church, or, as a compromise, that they may be permitted to indulge in the luxury of the new knowledge in every department of life except the religious life; that a dual personality is essential to religion? Or can the old faith influence men in the twentieth century as it did in the thirteenth and the fourth and the first? If the latter be admitted, there is hope for the unity of man's spiritual nature which will lead to a revival of the spiritual life.

II. THE SPIRIT OF MODERNISM

The origin of a name does not tell what a name later signifies. "The disciples were called Christians first in Antioch." It is thought by some that the name "Christian" was given in derision; the Jews wished it to be believed that the disciples were simply proclaiming a new form of the "Mystery" religions. Perhaps the Jews believed this. If so, the disciples could not have been pleased with the new name, but it stuck. In the same way, progressive Protestants may not like the contemptuous term "Modernist" but they must make the best of it. They must do what the disciples did—make the name worthy of respect. The first step must be taken by removing misunderstandings.

If we asked the average Fundamentalist what he understands by "Modernist," he probably would say that Modernists fail to recognize that the Church must have some foundation, and that their critical examination of the New Testament shows a spirit of irreverence which will ultimately lead to a denial of the historic Jesus.

The first question which the Modernist should ask is: On what is such an opinion based? If it be based on books or articles written by what used to be called "Free Thinkers" or by men who have abandoned the communion of the Church, it will be evident that an injustice is done to "Modernists" who are in the communion of the Church. In this discussion it is well to bear in mind in what sense the term "Modernist" is used by the present writer. It means communicants of the Church, and is represented by such a publication as the English *Modern Churchman* and such well-known scholars in England as its editor, the Rev. D. A. Major, Dean Rashdall,* Dean Inge, Archdeacon Wil-

* Alas, no longer living.

son, Canon Barnes, Canon Glazebrooke, Dr. Bethune-Baker, Dr. Mathews, Dr. W. R. Sorley, Prof. Percy Gardner, and the late Cyril W. Emmet, not to mention men of like standing and devotion in the Protestant churches of America. If the writings of such men be examined, it will be seen at once that there is grave misunderstanding in regard to what constitutes Modernism in the Church.[7]

That there must be some historical fact on which the Church is based, the Modernist will agree, but he believes that there is confusion in regard to what constitutes a foundation. His complaint is that the Fundamentalist has insisted that things belonging to the building which are evidently ornaments, conveniences, pinnacles, finishing the structure, are the foundations of the building. But the Fundamentalist, on the other hand, says: "If you once begin to touch anything on the building, it cannot fail that sooner or later you will be obliged to remove the corner-stone, and all this investigation of the meaning of the building and its growth will lead to its destruction." I profoundly sympathize with the fear of the Fundamentalist.

There are numbers of devout and earnest Christian men and women—I suppose the majority in all the churches—who are saying to themselves, "The end of all this controversy will be that men will cease to believe in the reality of the earthly life of Jesus Christ. We already hear voices proclaiming that the Gospel story has no historical value at all; that Jesus never lived; that he is simply the imaginary nucleus about which certain myths have clustered."

If this be Modernism, I would repudiate it as strongly as any Fundamentalist does. But it is not the logical result of Modernist thought, and it is never fair to judge a movement by the eccentrics who may seem to be associated with it. No Fundamentalist would think that justice were done him if Brother Jasper were quoted as a typical Fundamentalist with his celebrated dictum, "The sun do move." Every revolving sphere has a tendency to throw off particles at a tangent. There is a tendency in all stable governments towards despotism; there is a tendency in democracy towards anarchy. But who would think that it was a just description of any democratic country—America, England,

France—to say that the anarchists represent the real purpose of the men who believe in a republic? There is not a sane man who would not say, "They are the extravagant—the eccentric. They are not the fruit but the disease of democracy."

The same is true of the "Christ myth." It it not the logical result of the movement called Modernism. It is not the fruit of the critical historical examination which scholars have been carrying on for the last fifty years. It is a disease. Those who are familiar with the writings of sane scholars in England and America cannot fail to recognize that in this, as in other questions, the American churches are about a generation behind the English Church. The English scholars are through with this question and will no more give time to its consideration than a mechanical engineer would waste his time talking to a man who declared that he had in his satchel a model of a machine of perpetual motion. They know that it is simply one of the extravagances of human thought, and that it will not bear examination.

All men who have studied the history of the Church in the second and third centuries recognize that what are called the "Mystery" religions did influence the ritual and the creeds or theology of the Church, but to say that these were "displaced by a Christ myth" can only be met by such an argument as Archbishop Whately's clever skit called "Historic Doubts Relative to Napoleon Bonaparte." When Pitt rolled up the map of Europe after the battle of Austerlitz, he did not roll it up because the national bounds had been changed by an idea or by a myth, but because they had been changed by an idea incorporated in the life of a man, Napoleon Bonaparte.

The Roman Empire was not dominated by a myth. It was converted by the Gospel of the Man Christ Jesus who "in the days of Herod the king was *born*." The whole question has been summed up by Sir James Frazer, perhaps the greatest living authority on "myths": "The doubts which have been cast on the historical reality of Jesus are in my judgment unworthy of serious attention. Quite apart from the positive evidence of history and tradition, the origin of a great religious and moral reform is inexplicable without the personal existence of a great reformer. To dissolve the founder of

Christianity into a myth, as some would do, is hardly less absurd than it would be to do the same for Mohammed, Luther, and Calvin. Such dissolving views are for the most part the dream of students who know the great world chiefly through its pale reflection in books."[8] The historic reality of the Man Christ Jesus is the corner-stone of the Christian Church. On that, both Fundamentalists and Modernists can agree, but many do not recognize that while a *historic* church requires a *historic* foundation, *religion* antedates history.

The historic fact of the life of Jesus is not the foundation of *religion*. Religion existed before Jesus and it will exist if the Christian Church should disappear, for religion is that effort of the spirit of man to adjust itself to the mystery of this universe which appears as soon as man stands upright on this earth, and will continue until the last man has disappeared. But the Christian Church is a particular form of the religious life and is based upon the historic reality of the life of Jesus.

Not only is there a misapprehension as to the results of the critical study by the Modernist, but the purpose of the Modernist in this study is misunderstood. It is not idle curiosity which has led to the critical examination of the Gospel record; still less is it the manifestation of a spirit of scepticism. It is the spirit of men engaged in research in the hope that they may discover ways of helping suffering humanity. It is because the Modernist believes that the reality of the historic Jesus has been obscured by the mists of theological speculation that he is desirous of finding, if possible, what is the bed-rock fact in the Gospel narratives. He recognizes that we have in the record a reflection of the opinions of the writers and that sometimes those opinions are identified with the teachings of Jesus. If it is possible to find the historical fact embedded in these Gospels, the Modernist believes that the foundation stone on which the Christian Church is built will be revealed—which can be none other than Christ Jesus.

Unless this can be done, the Church will be driven to the scepticism of St. Augustine, who said, "I would not believe the Gospel but for the authority of the Church." That we owe to the Church the preservation of the documents which form the Bible is true, but the Church is not the authority on which we believe the revelation contained in those Gospels. It is only the witness to the prevailing influence of those truths on the lives of the generations that have followed. The Church is indeed the witness to but it is not the judge of truth.

The critical examination of the records is due to an effort to reveal the historic Jesus. If that work is not done by the disciples of Jesus and is left to those who have never felt the influence of his spirit, he will be relegated to the company of Buddha, Confucius, or Mohammed. But if it is possible to come face to face with that sublime Person and then find what influence he produced upon the minds and hearts of the men and women who came in contact with him, we, too, may receive the gift of his Spirit. But if we simply accept him and the record produced by the influence of his Spirit upon the first disciples because the Church declares that he existed and that the words which those men spoke are true, it will be impossible for the Protestant churches to continue. Religious men will be driven by the spirit of scepticism to abandon all intellectual effort and submit to an external infallible authority. That this submission will have advantages may readily be admitted. It will take from men the burden of the responsibility of answering the question which Jesus asked of the first disciples, "What think ye of Christ?" But the lifting of the responsibility will destroy the privilege which the Reformation revealed: that it is possible for the individual soul to enter into such communion with Christ as to be able to say, "We know him whom we have believed." If the historic Jesus is the foundation of a historic society, the personal communion of the soul with Christ is the foundation of that spiritual experience of which the Church is the outward and visible sign.

CHAPTER II

THE SUPERNATURAL AND MIRACULOUS

I. THE SUPERNATURAL

A second misunderstanding of the Modernist position is shown by the assertion frequently made by Fundamentalists that not only does the Modernist deny the supernatural, but that his scepticism concerning the supernatural is the final cause of his objection to miracles.[1]

The Modernist does not deny the supernatural, though he does think that it is an unfortunate and misleading word. He does not accept the old dualism which divided religion into "revealed" and "natural." He does not believe that there is such a thing as "natural" religion. He believes that all religion is supernatural; that is, that it is the result of the communion of the soul with the Spirit of the universe, which we call God. He does not think that religion is an illusion or that it is an invention of man. He believes it to be God's revelation of Himself through human experience. He conceives the whole universe to be the revelation of the Invisible God. He rejoices in St. Paul's great saying, "The invisible things of him from the creation of the world are clearly seen, being understood by the things that are made, even his eternal power and Godhead." He believes that man, being made in the image of God, has within him that which is akin to God, and that this Divine element seeks God as the magnet seeks the pole. He believes that God has spoken in divers ways and manners to the fathers and that He is speaking to us, His children, to-day. All this is superhuman—supernatural if one prefer that word, though spiritual is a still better word—for both man and nature are the expression of the Eternal Spirit, the Background and the Source of all that is revealed by the senses, by reason, and by imagination which in its highest form we call "faith," —that is, the power of seeing the invisible.

This is well expressed by Emerson: "But when, following the invisible steps of thought, we come to inquire, Whence is matter? and Whereto? many truths arise to us out of the recesses of consciousness. We learn that the highest is present to the soul of man; that the dread universal essence, which is not wisdom, or love, or beauty, or power, but all in one, and each entirely, is that for which all things exist, and that by which they are; that spirit creates; that behind nature, throughout nature, spirit is present; one and not compound it does not act upon us from without, that is, in space and time, but spiritually, or through ourselves; therefore, that spirit, that is, the Supreme Being, does not build up nature around us, but puts it forth through us, as the life of the tree puts forth new branches and leaves through the pores of the old. As a plant upon the earth, so a man rests upon the bosom of God; he is nourished by unfailing fountains, and draws at his need inexhaustible power."[2]

But if any should suppose that the acceptance of this statement would lead to pantheism, he might do well to consider these words of one who is not only a theist but also a devout member of the Roman Catholic Church: "No experiences are so real, none, in a way, are so well understood by the experiencing soul, as are its supernatural experiences. By supernatural, we here mean nothing preternatural, nothing even essentially miraculous, nothing that men, who are at all complete according to man's supernatural call and awakeness, cannot, or do not, experience. . . . And, again, this Supernaturalness does not concern Goodness alone, but also Truth and Beauty. God is the Fountain and the Fullness, the Origin and the End, the ultimate Measure of every kind and degree, as much of Beauty and Truth as of Goodness."[3]

"We are busy here, not with the Miraculous, but with the Supernatural. When Bossuet and Fénelon had their celebrated controversy, Fénelon . . . insisted against Bossuet . . . that the entire spiritual life, from its rudimentary beginnings up to its very highest grades and developments, was for him, Fénelon, essentially and increasingly supernatural, but at no point essentially miraculous. . . . With Fénelon we will not deny the possibility, or even the actual occurrence of miracle, in the sense just indicated, *within the spiritual life.** Still less will we deny *historically attested** miracles in the Bible and elsewhere. But we will simply hold with Fénelon that the spiritual life of Prayer, of Love, and of Devotedness is, even in its fullest Christian developments, essentially not miraculous, but supernatural."[4]

*Italics mine.

II. THE MIRACULOUS

This distinction between the supernatural and the miraculous is, as I understand it, the position taken by the Modernist. He believes in the supernatural; that in God and in God alone we live and move and have our being. He does not deny *historically attested* "miracles," but what he does deny is the assertion that miracles are the supreme evidences of the supernatural; in other words, that life in general is separated from God, but that from time to time God reveals Himself in some abnormal and startling way. He says with Wordsworth:

"There was a time when meadow, grove, and stream,
The earth, and every common sight,
To me did seem,
Apparelled in celestial light."

When such thoughts fill our minds, we are moving in the atmosphere of mysticism, the primal and essential element in religious experience. But a historic religion requires us to place our feet on the earth and deal with the history of the Church exactly as we deal with any other history, not to react from mysticism into scepticism, but in order to understand the mind and heart of religious men of old. That they believed in miracles cannot be denied. The record is found both in the Old and in the New Testament, and we are sure that to the men of old miracles were the witnesses to the presence of God in human life.

When Matthew Arnold said, "Miracles do not happen," he was identifying "miracle" with the "overruling of nature by the author of nature." Miracles do happen if by "miracles" we mean inexplicable events. The whole history of mankind records such "miraculous" events. But inasmuch as they are part of a historical record, they must be tested by historical criteria. In other words, while miracles are not to be denied because of any *a priori* theory, on the other hand they are not to be accepted unless the "historic evidence" is clear and convincing.

This, then, is the question: Have the "miracles" recorded in the Bible convincing historic evidence? But when the question is so put, many Fundamentalists refuse to allow it to be so considered, "because," they say, "these events being recorded in an infallible Book are not to be tested as the stories in Herodotus or any other secular history are tested—by critical examination. They must be accepted as part of an inerrant Divine revelation." This, of course, is the position of those Fundamentalists who deny that the larger knowledge of nature associated with what is called the law of evolution, should be taught to Christian people, because it is evident that if the truth discovered by the study of nature be accepted, it is brought at once into conflict with the revelation in the Bible. Of course, no intelligent Fundamentalist accepts this dogma with all its implications, for that would mean that when he says, "From the rising of the sun unto the going down of the same" he believes that this earth is a plane; that the firmament is a fixed vault; and that the sun moves around the earth and not the earth around the sun. But when it comes to definite statements of what are supposed to be facts: that the earth was created in the way described in the book of Genesis; that a certain man and a certain woman lived in a garden; that a serpent spoke to the woman; that a man commanded the sun to stand still and it stood still; that an ass rebuked a prophet; that an axehead floated; that a dead child was brought to life by a prophet; that a man lived for three days in the belly of a great fish—all these things being a part of the Divine record may not be called in question. But the result has been that multitudes of men and women who would not accept the dogma and are convinced that these wonderful stories are simply the natural expression of the psychological atmosphere which the men of old were breathing, are debarred from all the spiritual nourishment that is contained in the ancient record.

And yet there is a famine, "not a famine of bread, nor a thirst for water, but of hearing the word of God." The word of God is in that Old Testament, but it came to and through men who could only express that word in accordance with the intellectual categories in which alone thought to them was possible. Great numbers who call themselves Fundamentalists have been driven to admit this as far as the Old Testament is concerned, but they decline to allow a critical examination of the New Testament because they are afraid that an explanation of the marvellous events recorded there would destroy faith in the revelation of the Son of God. But some one is going to examine the records and tell the result of that examination, so that the real problem is, Who is to study critically the New Testament? The Modernists believe that it should be done by members of the Church, and they are trying to do it. They are asking, "What is the historical evidence for the wonderful stories related in the New Testament?" They are not seeking to eliminate miracles from the New Testament record. They are simply asking for the historical evidence on which belief in these miracles is based. It is apparent that less evidence is needed for those abnormal events, such as the casting out of devils and the healing of the sick by a word or a touch, than is needed to prove such marvels as walking upon the waters or multiplying loaves and fishes. It is not sufficient to say that an Omnipotent God can do whatever He pleases. It is our humble duty to try and learn what an Omnipotent God has willed to do. Indeed, the whole conception of Omnipotence needs to be carefully re-examined. To assert that God, because He is Omnipotent, can do anything, cannot mean that He can violate the moral law which He has revealed to man, so that what is unjust in man is just in God, what is untrue in man is true in God. He cannot tell a lie; He cannot make two and two to be five—which simply means that He does not will to do these things. They would be the denial of His own nature. The question is, What has He done in regard to the universe which is the expression of His will? There is no reason to believe that He ever intends to violate the laws by which this universe moves.

If the healing of the sick by a word seems to be a violation of law, we are driven to consider whether we have not made a false diagnosis; in other words, whether there is not psychical as well as physical law. It may be that the day will come when it shall seem to be as natural to walk on the waters or multiply loaves and fishes as it now seems to heal the sick in the way the Gospel declares that they were healed in the day of Jesus. But that will be to eliminate miracles not by denying them but by understanding them. In other words, they will cease to be miracles, that is, inexplicable events.

The Modernist, then, is examining the records to ask what the evidence is for certain inexplicable events. If he find that evidence insufficient, he cannot state that he believes the event to have been a physical occurrence, and is led to ask what was the psychological atmosphere in which such marvellous stories originated, and then endeavor to find out what is the spiritual significance which those marvellous stories embody. In all this he may be wrong but he is not denying the supernatural.

If this were clearly understood, we should hear no more that the Modernist is obsessed by scientific dogmatism. On the contrary, I believe that it will be found that the Modernist would be in agreement with such a statement as this: "The universality of natural law is no more than a very big generalization resting upon a long series of observations; if any facts to the contrary can be surely established, the generalization is thereby disproved. We have no *a priori* certainty of this 'reign of law.' . . . Let but one miracle be proved, and we must revise this conception of the universal life as an unbroken web of uniformities. . . . But whether this be the case or not we cannot determine *a priori;* we must simply sharpen our observation, keep our eyes open for evidence."[5] But in seeking to escape from scientific dogmatism, the Fundamentalist is in danger of falling into that opposition to scientific method which has led to such direful results in the past.[6]

If, now, we turn to the evidence, we may be led to conclude that the non-scientific atmosphere in which the writers of the New Testament lived was conducive to belief in the miraculous. We must recognize that in this day "while the evidence for natural laws has been growing steadily greater, the evidence for miracles has been growing as steadily less. Remote and credulous times are full of miracles; we hear of them but rarely, if at all, to-day. They flourish in the dark and vanish with the light of day" [like the ghost of Hamlet's father they fade away at the crowing of the cock, which announces the dawn of day], "with the growth of the habit of accurate observation and recording of observations. They seem to have an affinity for uncultivated minds and superstitious habits of thought; we do not find them entering into the experience of the educated. No single case of what would clearly be a miracle has ever been vouched for by such careful scientific observation as to leave no room for doubt of the facts. Even if we had apparently unimpeachable evidence, in some isolated instance, of a fact which, if it existed, would be a miracle, we should have to bear in mind the great fallibility of human testimony, and reserve our acquiescence until it had been corroborated by testimony from other observers or in other similar cases."[7]

I believe that the reason so many devout people feel it essential to maintain a belief in miracles is due to the fact that they believe the miracles were the protest against a mechanistic theory of the universe which was prevalent in the third quarter of the nineteenth century. But no such necessity exists to-day, because the whole tendency of the scientific conception of the universe has changed and become more spiritual.[8] What will ultimately be the effect of the more spiritual interpretation of the universe no one is in a position to-day to say. In regard to this matter, it would be well to avoid on the one hand the spirit of credulity, and on the other the spirit of scepticism. A reverent agnosticism in regard to such questions is the attitude of the best religious minds to-day. The fact is, we know very little. If there were any one fact in the universe absolutely known, the whole universe would be known:

> "Flower in the crannied wall,
> I pluck you out of the crannies,
> I hold you here, root and all, in my hand,

Little flower—but *if* I could understand
What you are, root and all, and all in all,
I should know what God and man is."

If, then, with an open mind we turn to the record of "miraculous" events in the New Testament, we shall find that not only were these events recorded by men whose minds scientifically were childlike—that is, who like a child conceived the possibility of anything's happening—but we may be led to conclude that the time has come when, like St. Paul, we should put away childish things, and find that there is no loss but great gain. Now, one of the childish things which the study of primitive man has revealed is that, whether "magic" preceded "religion" or "religion" "magic," the two were intimately connected. There are many devout men who believe that "miracles" are but vestiges of primitive "magic."

Turning to the record we find, first of all, that the Western mind is essentially prosaic, while the Oriental mind is poetic. So we value "the irresistible force of understatement." But the Oriental mind fails to feel the force of carefully guarded prose, and expresses itself in poetic hyperbole. Where we should say, "I am compelled by my conscience to refrain from such or such an action," the Oriental says, "I am forbidden by the voice of God." The scientific mind deals with secondary causes or immediate antecedents, while the Oriental disregards the immediate antecedents and finds in every event the immediate activity of God. The question is not, Which is the truer statement of fact? but whether the Western mind is justified in interpreting the Oriental hyperbole as if it were a statement of fact.

Secondly, we find that there is a process of growth in the miraculous stories. For example, an event recorded in St. Mark's Gospel is expanded and becomes more and more marvellous in the Gospels of St. Matthew or St. Luke.

Then, too, not a few of the so-called miracles appear to be dramatic forms of what were originally parabolic statements, such as the blasting of the fig-tree, which may be no more than the allegoric presentation of Jesus' prophecy of the fate of the unfruitful tree in the parable.

Fourth, we cannot fail to be impressed by the fact that if the incidents of the marvellous stories recorded in the Gospels actually took place, so little impression should have been made by them upon the contemporaries of Jesus; that when they called for just such signs, Jesus not only refused to give them but declared that the craving for them was a sign of the weakness of faith.

A fifth point, which it is very difficult for us to appreciate to-day, is this: that in early days, men felt no such obligation as every historian feels to-day, to record fact as fact and poetry as poetry. If any saying was illuminating and inspiring, ancient authors did not hesitate to illustrate the truth by a dramatic story. The whole attitude concerning literary morality has completely changed, though traces of the earlier feeling can be found in the uncritical histories of every nation. Parson Weyman's history of Washington's early life, it is generally recognized to-day, is an untrustworthy guide as far as facts are concerned, though it is illuminating as illustrating the fundamental principles of the "Father of his Country." The story of the cherry-tree, which the children of fifty years ago received as historic fact, is now recognized to be a parable by which the truthfulness of Washington is illustrated. The writer did not feel that he was telling a lie; he recorded the tradition without examination, as an illustration of the truth he desired to impart. This, I believe, is true of all early historians, whether of Greece or of Rome or of Israel.

But this is only the negative side of the question. There are positive difficulties in the way of accepting the miraculous stories as literal history. Men feel to-day, as was not felt fifty years ago, that a wonderful event is no proof of the *character* of the miracle worker. The wonder might have been performed by a malign spirit, as was suggested by the enemies of Jesus.

Secondly, that one life should have been relieved from the inevitable consequences of natural law, while the great majority still suffered, leads to a thought of favoritism on the part of God which strikes at the very root of belief in His Fatherhood. If the beautiful story told in St. Luke's Gospel is to illustrate the sympathy shown to the widow of Nain and the assurance brought to her by Jesus of eternal life, in which there shall be no more parting or tears, we have a revelation of the continuing sympathy and enlightenment which Jesus brings to every mourning soul. But when it is crystallized into an exceptional act, it brings no comfort to the widow to-day bereaved of her only child.

And, above all, the modern mind has been led to feel that the identification of religion with the acceptance of marvellous events degrades religion from a supreme spiritual experience to an acceptance of belief in a non-rational universe. So there are many who feel that insistence upon miracles is deadening to the expansion of faith.

If, now, in conclusion, we look back to the results which have followed from the critical examination of the Bible, who can fail to see how great the gain has been? As long as every word in the Old Testament was believed to be the expression of the eternal truth spoken by God Himself, every line in that ancient record became a law, a law like that of the Medes and Persians, which could not be altered. I have heard that when anæsthetics were first employed by gynecologists, there were devout women who refused to receive them, and so allay the pangs of childbirth, because of the word in the book of Genesis which condemned women to bring forth children in sorrow. The declaration that "whoso sheddeth man's blood, by man shall his blood be shed" for a long time prevented even the consideration of the abolition of capital punishment. Religious men did not feel themselves at liberty to consider whether or not it was best for the people to abolish a practice which may be deterrent but has unquestionably led to the execution of the innocent. "It is written," and that closed the door to any possibility of reform. Some of us can remember that in our youth slavery was not only justified by an appeal to the supposed curse upon Cainan and his descendants, but was actually preached in the Christian pulpits, as a necessary condition for the perpetuation of the eternal will of God. Fortunately, none of us is old enough to remember the horrors that followed because of the belief that a witch should be not suffered to live. But the history of New England reveals the horrors that followed from the obedience to the letter.

Now, when in addition to these considerations we recognize the great light that has been thrown upon the evolution of religion as illustrated in the gradual growth in the knowledge of God, in the long story of the seeking of the lost soul recorded in the Old Testament, in the gradual unfolding of the vision of the ideal life which God in the fulness of time would reveal, we recognize that we have passed from the slavery of the letter into that freedom of the spirit which has made the Old Testament a means of strengthening and refreshing the soul. Why should it be supposed that other benefits would not arise if the religious life could be emancipated from "the letter that killeth" in the New Testament also, and so enter into the spirit that gives life. There are multitudes, and as the years go on the multitudes will increase, of intelligent boys and girls, young men and women, who are kept from entering into the fellowship of Jesus because the knowledge of the universe which they believe to be the revelation of the wisdom and goodness and beauty of God cannot be reconciled with the dogmas that have been associated with those sacred writings which bring us into the presence of the Divine Man, and show us the influence of the Spirit of God upon those who receive Him. It is due to such considerations as these that the Modernist feels that the Church is making a fatal mistake in identifying religion with acceptance of the miraculous, for if the revelation of God in the Bible be dependent upon the acceptance of miracles, and the study of nature leads to scepticism of the miraculous, we may find that students of nature are led to deny the very existence of God.

CHAPTER III

THE TWO SUPREME "MIRACLES"

Just as there are many in the Episcopal Church who have abandoned the obscurantist attitude of the Fundamentalist in regard to the Old Testament, so are there many who, while they are not willing to call themselves Modernists, for thereby it might be concluded that they were in sympathy with certain extravagances associated in the popular mind with Modernism, yet fear that they may ultimately be driven by an inexorable logic to apply the same methods to the New Testament which they have been led to apply to the Old. For there are two records in the New Testament of such supreme importance that they feel it necessary to make a stand there, and refuse to admit that there can be any discussion in regard to the method of the resurrection or the birth of our Lord. It will be better, then, in considering the problems of the Episcopal Church to drop the word "Fundamentalist" and substitute Traditionalist or Conservative.

It will not do for the Modernist to assert that

this attitude of mind is illogical. That is to overlook the fact that reason is but one of the elements in personality, and that its importance as a guiding principle of life has been greatly exaggerated. When men's emotions are deeply stirred, they decline to be dominated by the tyranny of logic. There is profound truth in the much misunderstood dictum of Tertullian, "I believe because it is incredible." The Resurrection and the Incarnation may seem incredible, but they are essential foundations of Christian faith. St. Paul's statement is as true today as when he wrote to the Corinthians, "If Christ be not raised, your faith is vain; ye are yet in your sins," and so is that statement in the first Epistle of St. John, "Every spirit that confesseth not that Jesus Christ is come in the flesh is not of God."

Here is common ground on which all Christians stand. But when it is suggested that there may have been a misunderstanding as to the method, both of the Resurrection and of the Incarnation, it is not strange that the Traditionalist should not only be alarmed but that he should be filled with righteous indignation, and suppose that those who wish to examine the record and re-interpret its message are the enemies of Christ and his Church. If this is borne in mind, the Modernist will be enabled "when he is reviled, not to revile again"; all the charges of dishonesty, of irreverence, of lack of faith, will be interpreted as exhibitions of the zeal of men and women to whom the Incarnate and Risen Lord is the one supreme object of love and adoration.

Nevertheless, when it is asserted that the doctrines of the Virgin Birth and the "bodily" Resurrection of our Lord are historic facts, they must be tested by historic criteria. And when they are examined it may be found that some of the difficulties which are clearly present to the mind of the Modernist, but are suppressed doubts in the mind of the Traditionalist, will be cleared away and the way opened so that men can say to-day with St. John, "The Word was made flesh, and dwelt among us, and we beheld his glory, the glory as of the only begotten of the Father, full of grace and truth," and with St. Paul, "And last of all he was seen of me also." In this spirit let us reverently open the Scriptures and consider first the story of the Resurrection.

I. THE RESURRECTION OF JESUS

The first effect of this examination will doubtless be confusing. Sometimes it would seem as if we were in the presence of a natural body which has been re-animated, and at other times it seems as if we saw a ghost. If it be asserted that the "bodily" resurrection of our Lord is a historic fact, we are obliged to ask what is meant by "bodily." The ordinary interpretation would lead us to suppose that it meant a physical body. If, however, it means a "spiritual" body, there is no problem. But it is not to be forgotten that St. Paul makes a sharp contrast between *pneuma*, "the spirit," and *sarx*, "the flesh"—"The 'spirit' is certainly something not fleshly, not earthly, not material."[1] If, then, "bodily" resurrection means that the body which was laid in the tomb was re-animated, the historic evidence for that fact is more than doubtful. But if it means that Jesus revealed himself in the supreme personality which emerged after the experience of death, we are on sure ground. "The Easter experiences of St. Peter and others . . . can never be completely analyzed by historical means, but the substance of them is described by men and women in like manner: Jesus appeared to them in divine glory as the One whom God had raised from the dead, with words of encouragement and promise upon His lips.

"These experiences of the apostles are the psychological starting-point of the earliest cult of Jesus in Palestine, the *sine qua non* for the growth and organization of Christian churches. . . . They invested the form of the Messiah with the resplendence of Deity itself, turned the torturing problem of the Cross into a miracle of grace, opened the sacred writings of the old prophetic period and roused up new confessors and prophets in a great revival."[2]

In the fifteenth chapter of the First Epistle to the Corinthians it is stated that Christ "was buried and that he rose again the third day according to the Scriptures." If that were all that St. Paul told us, I think we should have to conclude that he believed that the body which was laid in the tomb was re-animated and appeared on the third day. But when we come to the examination of that appearance of Christ which St. Paul experienced, we see that there is no indication of any "body."

The story is told twice in the Acts of the Apostles, written, as we believe, by St. Luke, the companion of St. Paul. These two accounts are found in the ninth and the twenty-second chapters. They both declare the shining of a great light and the hearing of a voice. The light "above the brightness of the sun" was the *Shekinah*, the illumination of the Divine glory, and the voice was the voice of the Word of God. In one account we are told that Saul's companions heard the voice but saw no man; and in the other that they saw the light but heard not the voice. This seems to indicate that the appearance was to Saul alone. In modern language this is called a psychological experience. Whether there was any physical phenomenon we cannot be sure. What we are sure of is that this man Saul knew that he was in the presence of the Son of God.

It is also to be remembered that St. Paul states distinctly that our resurrection is to be like the Resurrection of Christ: "He that raised up Christ from the dead shall also quicken your mortal bodies by his spirit that dwelleth in you." As long as it was believed that every Christian body laid in the grave would appear at the last day, there was no difficulty in supposing that the natural body of Jesus had appeared on the third day. But when men became convinced that their own bodies would not rise, they were led to ask whether St. Paul believed that the physical body of our Saviour had been re-animated. If his Resurrection differed essentially from our own, the whole argument of St. Paul falls to the ground.

When we turn to the Synoptic Gospels we find, to our infinite regret, that the last chapter of the earliest Gospel, that of St. Mark, has come to us in mutilated form. It ends with the eighth verse of the sixteenth chapter, and the concluding verses have been added from St. Matthew's Gospel. We have, then, only the story of the angelic vision, but no account of the appearance of the Lord. But inasmuch as the angel's message is to Peter, we may conclude that St. Mark's Gospel ended with an account of the appearance to which St. Paul refers in Corinthians: "He was seen of Cephas, then of the twelve: After that, he was seen of above five hundred brethren at once. . . . After that, he was seen of James; then of all the apostles. And last of all he was seen of me also."

In the Gospel of St. Matthew, as the women turned from the tomb to fulfill the angel's message to the disciples, Jesus met them and they held him by the feet. Note that this is the first suggestion of a "body." But when he appears to the eleven disciples on a mountain in Galilee, we are told that "when they saw him, they worshipped him: but some doubted." This appearance seems to imply a "vision," but no corporeal materialization.

In St. Luke's account there is the appearance of angels, but no appearance to the women nor even to St. Peter, who goes to the sepulchre. Jesus appears to two disciples on their way to Emmaus, and here we have an account of a conversation which causes the hearts of the disciples to burn within them as the unknown companion unfolds to them the meaning of the Scriptures. But it was not until the "breaking of bread" that "he was known of them." There are many who believe that this account reflects a later experience of the Church communing with the living Lord in the study of the Scriptures and in the celebration of the Sacrament.

When we turn to the Fourth Gospel, we read

the story of the appearance to Mary Magdalene, which she supposes to be that of the gardener, indicating a corporeal presence. And that is deepened by the story of Thomas, who "sees in his hands the print of the nails, and puts his finger into the print of the nails, and thrusts his hand into his side," and again, by Jesus' appearance to Peter by the lakeside, when he gives to the disciples bread and fish (a more highly developed sacramental suggestion) and talks with Peter just as familiarly as he had talked with him before the Crucifixion. Here it is seen that there is a steady progress from a vision of glory to a corporeal companionship. But it must not be overlooked that the writer of the Fourth Gospel declares that those who have not seen and yet have believed show evidence of greater faith than is revealed by the narrative of Thomas' experience.

Who can say which of these "appearances" is the one that must be accepted by a disciple to-day? We can quite understand the hesitation of those who are unwilling to abandon belief in a corporeal appearance, lest they should lose the reality. But that is to identify reality with the physical rather than with the spiritual.

Yet it may be asked, What assurance have we that the "vision" was not an illusion—a self-generated hallucination?[3] The answer is that the effects produced by the appearance to Saul were not the effects of hallucination. Those inevitably manifest themselves in excitement, irrational delusions, and weakening of the will. But with Paul, there is sanity; there is reason; there is inflexible will to accomplish a purpose revealed in and by the vision; and the same is true of all to whom Christ appeared.

Doubt as to the "bodily" Resurrection does not lead to scepticism as to the reality of the appearance. These appearances are judged, not by the reason of the "Free Thinker"; they are judged by the faith of a disciple, a disciple who is convinced that the full personality of Jesus was exalted to the presence of God, and that through that exaltation power was given to enter into communion with the soul that was seeking him. If we have faith in the supernatural, and believe that the manifestation of the risen life did not originate in the individual but was an effect produced by a real, that is, spiritual communion, we find ourselves in an atmosphere where it is not necessary to identify our faith either with a corporeal manifestation or a purely subjective "vision," but where faith is nourished by the conviction that not only were the souls of the first disciples illuminated, inspired, and directed by the Lord of life, but that the same experience so dramatically described in the early records may be in a measure participated in by the humblest Christian today.[4] So, as truly as Paul, the Christian may say, "Last of all he was seen of me also."

II. THE VIRGIN BIRTH

If the Traditionalist could free his mind from certain obsessions, he would be in a better position to understand the Modernist's attitude towards the doctrine of the Virgin Birth. The Modernist's hesitation to admit that the doctrine expresses a historic fact is not due, as is commonly supposed, to a denial of the supernatural or even of the possibility of a miracle. He devoutly recognizes the first and has no desire to dogmatize in regard to the second. His position has been finely stated by one of the greatest historians the Episcopal Church has produced: "It is to have been devoutly wished that the present controversy about the Virgin-birth had not arisen to disturb the peace of the Church. Many of those who feel keenly the modern difficulties would have preferred to allow objections to slumber, in the conviction that no serious issue was involved."[5] The Modernist, therefore, would say in the words of Elijah, "*I* have not troubled Israel."

The Modernist is not ignorant of the appeal which this doctrine makes to the devout spirit. He recognizes that the introduction to the history of Jesus is as beautiful and moving as Beethoven's Ninth Symphony.[6] He recognizes that it has been the inspiration of art and poetry and music. He knows that it has inspired thousands of men and women to turn away from the joys of the married life that they might devote themselves unhampered to the service of the Lord; that it was the sanctifying influence in that romantic movement called chivalry; that to the idealization of woman is largely to be attributed the glorious Gothic architecture, the crown of which is the "Lady Chapel."[7] He recognizes what an important place it has had in theology; how essential it seemed to those who believed in Original Sin, making guilty every soul born into the world by natural generation, that there should be faith in One Life that entered into the world in a way that escaped the curse. He recognizes that it emphasized the uniqueness of Jesus and was a protest against that "natural evolution" which seemed to make him but the flower and fruit of the growing human plant so that God was eliminated; that to many it seems not only congruous but essential that the Divine Life should have entered humanity by a stupendous miracle. It is therefore not surprising that the Traditionalist should suppose that any questioning of the Virgin Birth as a historic fact should lead to doubt as to the sinlessness, the uniqueness, and the divinity of our Lord—perhaps finally to the denial of Christ. Therefore, the Modernist would have preferred that the doctrine should not have been called in question but that emphasis should have been laid upon the sinlessness, the uniqueness, and the divinity of our Saviour in such a way that if the historic fact were doubted, the truth might remain unquestioned.

But the question is now before the Church and it behooves the Modernist to explain why it is that some who are so designated have been led to deny the historic fact. I say "some," for it should be remembered that denial of the historic fact is not the characteristic of Modernism. There are many pronounced Modernists who accept the doctrine as a historic fact. I have talked in the last thirty years with a large number of Modernist clergy in the Episcopal Church and I have met but one who dogmatically denied that the Virgin Birth was a historic fact, though many have declared that the evidence was not sufficient to justify them in dogmatically asserting that it was a historic fact. But what differentiates the Modernist from the Traditionalist is his estimate of the spiritual value of the fact. He does not consider it essential to belief in the Incarnation. He does not insist that it must be accepted by every Christian man or every Christian minister. His contention is that the man who believes that "Jesus Christ is come in the flesh" and desires to "follow him" and to make his way known amongst men, is a true Christian and a lawful minister of the Church.

I have said that the Modernist does not ignore the influence of the doctrine, but he has been led to question if those who lay such stress upon it have not assumed that the effects are due to a cause, while, as a matter of fact, the effects have largely produced the cause: in other words, that this argument is an example of the fallacy known in logic as *post hoc, ergo propter hoc*. If, for the moment, it be granted that the doctrine was not part of the original Evangelical tradition but was added later because it had come to be believed that virginity was a higher state than marriage, then it would follow that virginity must be ascribed to the mother of the Lord, or else it would have been supposed that He had not come "in the flesh" in the noblest way. If "Original Sin" be not a fact but a nightmare, then the reason which was once so potent in this doctrine is seen to have no force. That chivalry was inspired by this doctrine may be true, and yet it may be found that the doctrine did not originate it but that the idealization of woman was the spiritual contribution of the Teutonic heroes, who found in the doctrine an explanation of their belief which gave it a religious sanction.

But if the appeal be made to history, we must accept all that history has to tell and not only what is pleasing to us. While it was believed that the sinlessness of Jesus was witnessed to by this doctrine, it must not be forgotten that it was a potent means of clamping upon the Church that dreadful doctrine of Original Sin which darkened human life until the discoveries of Darwin led to the acknowledgment that the story of Adam and Eve was a myth. If the divinity was assured, it was also identified with miracle, which shows nothing of the character of the Divine, except power. That conception led to Deism and the final denial of the Incarnation.* If virginity was exalted, by the same measure was marriage discredited. If celibacy was declared to be the more perfect way—we know what that led to as shown by the history of monasticism.

Unquestionably it inspired the building of great cathedrals, but it is to be remembered that these cathedrals were not built for the worship of God the Father, nor even for the adoration of His Son. It was the worship of the Virgin which had become essential, because the humanity of Christ had been eliminated. There was

*The rise and progress of Unitarianism in New England, beginning as a protest against Jonathan Edwards' preaching of Original Sin, illustrates this.

need of a mediator who was essentially human, and that mediator was found in the tender-hearted Mother of God. In other words, the old Arian heresy, which taught that the one thing needful for salvation was a divinity which was not essentially the same as the divinity of the Father, was revived. So when the humanity of Christ had been eliminated and the Virgin substituted, men were really worshipping a sort of divinity, the divinity which they were attributing subconsciously to the Virgin and which consciously they would later be compelled to formulate in the doctrine of the Immaculate Conception. The obverse of the medal is not a thing in which the Church can take pleasure.

If, then, the doctrine of the Virgin Birth is no longer deemed essential for the sinlessness of our Lord (because the doctrine of Original Sin has been abandoned), and is no longer needed to prove the divinity of our Lord (because it is recognized that miracle cannot be the final proof of divinity), all that is left of its value is that it is supposed to witness to the uniqueness of our Saviour. But emphasis upon the physical fact can only lead to belief in physical uniqueness, and physical uniqueness is deformity. The doctrine, whether a historic fact or not, if unduly stressed, leads to a denial of the Perfect Humanity.[8]

But let it be understood that the examination of the evidence for the historic fact is not put forth to prove that the Traditionalist is wrong, but simply as an explanation of the way in which men who have endeavored to follow their ordination vow to "read diligently the Holy Scriptures, with the aid of such studies as help to a knowledge of the same," have been led to the conclusion that there has been a profound misunderstanding as to what the Scriptures teach. As I understand their position, they do not deny that certain verses in St. Matthew's and St. Luke's Gospels set forth the Virgin Birth as a historic fact. Their contention is that this represents a later tradition, and that there is an earlier tradition to be found by the careful study of the New Testament documents, and with that earlier tradition they find themselves in greater sympathy.

Most thoughtful people in the Episcopal Church, whether Modernists or Traditionalists, have abandoned the dogma of the inerrancy of the Scriptures, whether of the Old or New Testament. They no longer consider that every statement in them is unquestionably true. They have learned from the Collect for the second Sunday in Advent to ask help to "digest" the Holy Scriptures; that is, to eliminate what is not nourishing and to absorb that which gives life. One of the most scholarly of the Traditionalists calls attention to the fact that the Creed does not require "belief in the Feeding of the Five Thousand or the Raising of Lazarus as an essential article of faith. If one be brought by the examination of the records . . . to doubt the story of the Walking on the Sea, the Creeds . . . leave (him) free to do so."[9]

There is another point on which the Traditionalist and the Modernist are agreed, which is that the New Testament, as well as the Old, is not one book but a small library, made up of many books. These books are arranged in our Bibles not in chronological order but according to subjects, as books are arranged in every library. So to understand the thought of the early disciples, we must begin with the earliest records, which are St. Paul's Epistles.

In no one of these Epistles is there any allusion to the Virgin Birth. Now, while the argument from silence can never be conclusive, it seems to many minds simply incredible that if St. Paul knew the fact he should never have alluded to it. It is true that he came to the faith of Christ not through association with Jesus but by the revelation of the spiritual Christ risen from the dead. It is therefore natural that the great emphasis should have been laid by him upon the Resurrection, and that that should have led him back to the Cross, and that then the mind should have gone back to the institution of the Last Supper, where Jesus' death and "coming again" were prophesied. The birth as a historic fact is recognized, but between the birth and the institution of the Supper there is no allusion to the tradition later incorporated in the Synoptic Gospels. But that does not mean that Paul knew nothing about the ministry of the Lord Jesus, his teaching, the reality of the historic Person in whom, he says, "dwelt all the fulness of the Godhead bodily" (Colossians 2:9). He appeals to "words of the Lord Jesus" which are not recorded in the Gospels but were part of the current tradition.

But if St. Paul knew of this doctrine, it seems incredible that there should have been no mention of it in his preaching, of which we understand the Epistles give us the substance. If he did know it, the conclusion must be that he considered it of slight importance. But how could such a stupendous miracle be thought of slight importance? Bishop Gore concludes from the fact that St. Luke was St. Paul's companion that St. Paul must have known all about the birth of Jesus that St. Luke knew. This, of course, is an assumption that needs to be proved. He states that St. Paul's "faith in the radical sinlessness of Christ—sinlessness, I mean, not in fact only but in principle, inasmuch as Christ was the new man, the sinless source of a new manhood—would have made the idea very agreeable to him."[10] Unquestionably. Therefore we are surprised that if Paul did know all that St. Luke is supposed to have known, he should never have alluded to it in connection with his doctrine of the sinlessness of Christ and the sinfulness of the "natural" man.

So the student is led to a more careful examination of the text, to see what St. Paul has to say about the historic fact of the birth of Jesus. There are two passages in which he refers to this. The first is in Galatians 4:4, where he says that "Jesus Christ was made of a woman."[11] It is not strange that those who come to the reading of the Epistle through the atmosphere produced by the previous reading of two of the Gospels, should assume that St. Paul is here in harmony with St. Matthew and St. Luke; but every one familiar with that phrase knows that it means born as every one is born. Job says, "Man that is born of woman is of few days, and full of trouble" (Job 14 : 1). Our Lord himself says, speaking of John the Baptist: "Among them that are born of women there hath not arisen a greater than John the Baptist" (Matthew 11 : 11).

Again, in the Epistle to the Romans (1 : 3), Paul says: "Jesus Christ . . . was made of the seed of David according to the flesh." This seems to be a statement that he was *naturally* descended from David. If then we turn to the tables of genealogy used by the writers of the first and third Gospels, we find that while they differ widely, St. Matthew's table says that this is "the generation of Jesus Christ, the son of David," who was a descendant of Abraham; and then the descent is traced down to Joseph, "the husband of Mary, of whom was born Jesus, who is called Christ." When we turn to the table which St. Luke uses, it is significant that it is placed immediately after the account of the Baptism, when Jesus was declared to be the Son of God by the voice from heaven. In this table it is said that Jesus "was supposed to be the son of Joseph." That "supposed to be" must mean that that was the popular opinion, which the introduction to Luke's Gospel undertakes to show was wrong. If it was wrong, then both these genealogies contradict the text which follows.

Dr. Moffatt, in his version of the New Testament, translates Matthew 1 : 16: "Jacob, the father of Joseph, and Joseph (to whom the virgin Mary was betrothed), the father of Jesus who is called Christ." This translation is based upon the text of Von Soden, which some scholars are inclined to believe is not right at this point. It is not necessary here to discuss such a question, for which I am quite unfitted. But it should be recognized that there are many scholars of repute, not German radicals but American students of unquestioned orthodoxy and sober judgment, who are convinced that this is the true reading of the Gospel. They tell us that this text of Von Soden rests on three sets of witnesses: the Old Syriac Version in the Sinaitic form (which is the *oldest version of the New Testament in existence*), four old Latin manuscripts, and two Greek ones. If that reading should be generally accepted, then the testimony of the King James' translation at this point would be seen to have no value, because it would be recognized that it is not what Matthew wrote. The question has, of course, not been settled. But the acceptance of this reading by such a careful scholar as Dr. Moffatt indicates one of the reasons which have led the Modernist to question the historicity of the introduction to the first and third Gospels.

Turning to St. Mark's Gospel, generally believed to be the earliest of the Synoptics, there seems to be no reason to doubt the tradition which has come from Papias, that this Gospel was written by Mark to record the teaching of St. Peter. It begins with the sublime announcement, "The beginning of the Gospel of Jesus Christ, the Son of God." But there is no mention of a birth from a virgin; there is no mention of the birth at all, and it is quite proper for the Traditionalist to say, "St. Mark was at liberty to begin the story where he saw fit. Beginning with the baptism, there was no occasion for him to refer to the birth. Yet no one doubts that he believed in the birth. If he did not mention the birth, there was no need to allude to the manner of the birth. But that is no proof that he did not believe the birth to have taken place as the first and third Gospels declare." All this may be true. But it is surprising, if Mark did believe in the miraculous birth, that he should have stated that he was writing the *beginning* of the Gospel; in other words, that he should have left out that which undoubtedly would have been believed to add to the glory of the Son of God.

We have spoken of Mark as writing under the influence of Peter. But it is to be remembered that Mark had also been a disciple of Paul. Considering, then, that there is no mention of this stupendous miracle in the earliest Gospel, many students consider themselves justified in believing that St. Mark is writing from the standpoint of St. Paul, even when he is recording facts, unknown to St. Paul, of the earthly life of Jesus which had been imparted to him by St. Peter. But as St. Peter was the contemporary of St. Paul, the Modernist is inclined to believe that St. Peter also knew nothing of the Virgin Birth.

He then turns to the Fourth Gospel. He accepts the opinion of most scholars to-day, that this Gospel was not written, as was once supposed, by the Apostle John, but by some disciple in Ephesus who possibly knew the tradition of St. John's teaching but who wrote his Gospel for a definite purpose: "That ye might believe that Jesus is the Christ, the Son of God; and that believing ye might have life through his name." The Modernist believes that this Gospel, written at the very end of the first century or in the early part of the second, is the sublime expression of the Church, which believed that Jesus Christ was the son of God, and found life in that faith. Surely, one would expect the Virgin Birth to have had a place in such a glorification; but there is no allusion to it.

Now many scholars are convinced that this unknown writer was also a disciple of St. Paul, as, while he has adopted certain Alexandrian modes of thought, he is entirely in sympathy with St. Paul's conception of the Lord of Glory. It cannot be that a writer at the end of the first or the beginning of the second century had never heard of the Virgin Birth. He had before him the Gospels of Matthew and Luke, but he ignored the story of the birth. Why? Was it because the introductions had not at that time been added, or because he did not think the birth story significant? Here again the Modernist is not basing his opinion upon the argument from silence. He finds that the writer, in describing Nathanael's approach to Jesus and Jesus' sublime statement that he was the "ladder" of which Jacob had dreamed, the means by which the soul was to ascend from earth to God, declares that Philip, who brought Nathanael to the Saviour, tells him that Jesus is the son of Joseph. And the conclusion that the Modernist draws from all this study is that there was a time in the history of the primitive community when Jesus was preached as the Son of God, not alone without allusion to the Virgin Birth but by those who apparently either did not know the tradition or ignored it.

The Modernist then turns again to the first and third Gospels, and using the help of such studies as lead to a knowledge of the same, asks if both these Gospels did not originally begin, as Mark's did, with the baptism of John.[12] Working on that hypothesis, he examines the text to see if there are any indications of a reason which might have led an "editor" either to write these introductions in full or to modify them in such a way as to make them coincide with the popular belief at a later date than when the Gospels originally appeared. There are many difficulties which such a hypothesis must meet. The language is in accordance with the rest of the books, and the suggestion that they were inserted as late as the second century seems an arbitrary assertion.* But nevertheless there are many scholars of repute who are convinced that the definite statements contained in the first and third Gospels—that Jesus was born without the agency of a human father—are a later insertion worked into the earlier tradition.[13]

When they turn to St. Matthew's Gospel, they note that the writer states that Jesus was born of a virgin in fulfillment of an Old Testament prophecy. Of course, the ordinary reader

*The references to the Virgin Birth in the Epistles of St. Ignatius may have been drawn from the current tradition and not from the formal record in the Gospels of Matthew and Luke, as we now have them.

of his Bible who believes it to be an infallible record accepts all statements without questioning whether they contradict one another or not, and as long as he does not question, there is of course for him no problem. But inasmuch as many have noted that the tables of genealogy and the narrative contradict one another, scepticism as to the value of the whole New Testament cannot fail to trouble the believer. He may escape from his difficulty as the Roman Catholic does, by saying: "We not only have an infallible Book, but we have also an infallible guide. The Church will give an interpretation which shows that there is never a contradiction between two statements in the Bible."[14] But the Protestant recognizes that if that be once admitted, we shall inevitably be led back to the very condition which Jesus so strongly protested against—the tradition of the fathers interpreted by the scribes, which shut the door to the Kingdom of Heaven. The English Church escaped from the dilemma by asserting that the Scriptures must be interpreted by the aid of "sound scholarship." That did not mean that every reader of the Bible must be a scholar; it meant that the ordinary reader was to be helped in his understanding by scholars, not by ecclesiastical officials. But the ordinary man has neither the time nor the training which fits him for following the discussions of scholars, any more than he has the time or ability to follow the discoveries of physical science. He accepts certain conclusions and tries to see if they work.

What, then, are the conclusions which scholars have reached in regard to the first Gospel? To speak frankly, they have not yet reached definite conclusions. The subject is still under investigation but progress has been made. But I think that all who have given serious study to the problem are agreed that what we call St. Matthew's Gospel was not written by the Apostle, but bears his name because he probably made a collection of the "sayings of Jesus" which the unknown author used as one of his principal sources. In addition to these "sayings of Jesus," the Evangelist used the Gospel of Mark, substantially in the form in which we now have it. These two are the principal sources of the Gospel of Matthew.

When we come to the consideration of the first two chapters of Matthew, there is wide difference of opinion among scholars of repute. The

Traditionalist, as has been noted above, differs from the Fundamentalist inasmuch as he does not accept the dogma of the inerrancy of the Bible. This may seem inconsistent with the Traditionalist's veneration for tradition, for the Jews and the early Church and, later, both Catholics and Protestants were at one in their acceptance of the dogma. Fortunately, men refuse to submit to the tyranny of logic but find a way of escape.

The Traditionalist has found a phrase which satisfies him: "The integrity of Holy Scripture." He applies this to the question in dispute and insists that if words be taken at their face value, it will be seen that the Virgin Birth is a historic fact. If it were not, it would not be so stated in the Gospels. But when attention is called to the difficulties which arise from the study of the whole story, and he is asked for historic proof, he replies that he believes that the record in Matthew is based upon the testimony of Joseph and that the story in Luke came to the Evangelist from Mary herself. This may be true, but it is not proof. It is assumption; in other words, a clear begging of the question. And, what is more, it not only does not lessen the difficulties, but rather adds to them. Whether we turn to that part of the Gospels which is generally accepted as historical or to that which is not so clearly historical—the introduction—the question arises: Why did Joseph and his mother "marvel at those things which were spoken" by Simeon? (Luke 2 : 33). Would they have "wondered" had they known? Why did Mary speak of herself and "his father"? (Luke 2 : 48). When he said that he must be "about his father's business" how could they fail to "understand"? (Luke 2 : 49-50). Had Mary known the historic fact, could she have joined with his brethren in believing him to be mad? (Mark 3 : 30). Could he have said that those who did the will of God were as truly spiritually his mother as she who bore his body, had it been a historic fact that she had born him miraculously? (Matthew 12 : 46-50; Mark 3 : 31-35; Luke 8 : 19-21). These are difficulties which the dogma raises. Dogmatism never has quieted and never can quiet doubts.

Second, there are not a few who are convinced that these two chapters formed no part of the Gospel as it came from the hand of "Matthew."*

* In a former consideration of this question ("Intellectual Integrity") I stated that this opinion was held by "conservative" scholars. That was a mistake. Who is to decide what consti-

There are serious difficulties in the way of such a theory. In the first place, it arose when the Gospels were thought to be a product of the second-century and the "myth" had had time to originate and spread. It was also believed that the origin of the Birth Story was Gentile and not Palestinian. But the second-century theory has now been generally abandoned, and the Gentile origin of the story has not only to meet the objection of the great Harnack, but the study of the language shows that it has an Aramaic flavor which could not have been imported from a Gentile source. Yet in spite of those difficulties there are scholars of repute who are convinced that even if the Gospels were written in the first century and in Palestine, nevertheless the first two chapters of Matthew were added by a later hand. Indeed, they are inclined to think that later the Introductions were added to answer the demands of the Gentile Christians who desired to know what the early disciples were supposed to know of the infancy of the Lord.

Third, there are those who, while they are not

tutes a "conservative"? I prefer now to say that it is the opinion of not a few scholars of repute, both German and American.

willing to admit that the first two chapters have been added later, do think that the text has been "edited." They tell us that all scholars are agreed that the Gospel of Mark has been edited —that the last sixteen verses of the last chapter have been added from Matthew—because the Gospel of Mark came to the early Church in a mutilated form. They remind us that many scholars of various schools recognize that the confession of Peter contained in Mark is the authoritative statement, and that the fuller form given in Matthew, as well as the commission to Peter and the charge to baptize in the name of the Trinity, represent the reflection of a later day. "If, then," they say, "the end should have been so evidently edited, why should not the introduction also show additions by a later hand?"

But this is not proof. And therefore more cautious scholars are saying that inasmuch as it is now generally admitted that the Synoptics were written between the years seventy and ninety,* and the language is the same through-

* A careful consideration of what is known as Blaas' theory of the Western text of the book of Acts has led Harnack and certain other noted scholars to revise their opinion in regard to the date of the Synoptic Gospels, and has led them to the conclusion that all

out, we are not justified in saying that the Birth stories are later than the original Gospels. And yet many of those same men are convinced—like Harnack—that the Birth stories do not represent a historic fact, nor are they a part of the original Evangelical tradition. So they suggest that we look carefully at the text of Matthew and see if the origin of this story of the miraculous birth cannot be found in Palestine itself.

Now, the writer of the first chapter of Matthew distinctly states that our Saviour was born of a virgin in fulfillment of a prophecy (Isaiah 7:14). But when we examine the prophecy, we find that the Evangelist did not quote from the Hebrew but from a Greek translation, called the Septuagint. The Hebrew word which is translated "*parthenos*" in Greek and "virgin" in English is "*'almāh*," which means not a virgin, but a "young woman"[15] of marriageable age. The Hebrews had an entirely different word for "virgin," viz., "*bethūlāh*." So a careful examination of the prophecy shows that the

three of those Gospels were written before the fall of Jerusalem. This theory is set forth lucidly and attractively (if not convincingly) by Archdeacon Wilson.[16]

prophet was declaring that a young woman, possibly his own wife, would bear a child within a year or two, and that certain historical events connected with Damascus and Samaria would take place before the child was old enough to know the difference between good and evil—which things did come to pass. This child was to be called "Immanuel," meaning "God with us," because in a few years there would be a revelation of God's presence as the protecting power in Sion. Now the Evangelist, firmly convinced that Jesus was the real "Immanuel," that is, that in him God was seen to be with human life as never before, naturally concluded that he must have been born in the way he understood the prophet had declared Immanuel would be born. If the prophecy were to be fulfilled, that is, its full meaning brought to light, the child *must* be born of a virgin. The modern historian would not feel at liberty to say that a thing did take place because it ought to take place, but ancient writers had no such scruple, as we see in the history of every nation of the ancient world. But when we examine the prophecy on which the Evangelist relied, we see that he was misled by a faulty translation, and so the story passes out of the realm of history into mystic devotion.

When, now, we turn to Luke's Gospel, we learn that he carefully collected all available material before beginning his story. He was not satisfied with any of the current accounts of our Lord's life. None of them seemed to him to bring out a truth which he had learned from Paul, that Christ was a "light to lighten the Gentiles." He also tells the story of our Saviour's birth, but he does not, like Matthew, base it on prophecy. He ascribes it to a message of an angel, the birth of Jesus being more wonderful than that of John, which also had been announced by an angel. The preceding story of the birth of John, I think, throws light on this story of the nativity of our Lord, though I do not think attention has been called to it before. There are two stories in the Old Testament not unlike the account of the birth of John: Isaac, the heir of the covenant, the freeborn son, of whom St. Paul makes so much, had been miraculously born in accordance with the announcement of a heavenly visitor; Samuel, the great reformer, who laid the foundation of the Davidic kingdom, had also been miraculously born, in accordance with the message of an angel. How natural, therefore, it must have seemed to the religious soul, reflecting on the birth of the Perfect Son, the revealer of the Kingdom of God, that he should have been even more miraculously born and more wonderfully announced. If Luke found such a story current in Palestine in the day he began to collect the material for his Gospel, he could not have omitted it without marring the beauty of his "Hymn to the Nativity."

But when we come to consider the historical basis for the supposed fact, we must come to the study, not in a poetical but in a critical mood. There are but two verses in Luke which are incompatible with the theory that our Lord was born in wedlock. If these two verses were omitted—which would not affect the continuity of the narrative—we should pass out of poetry into history.

But what right has any man so to mutilate the text? None at all. Nevertheless we are compelled to ask if those verses express what one would expect from the writings of Luke? He had been the companion of Paul. If Paul did not know this story; if the words of Paul which have already been quoted seem to exclude it, is it likely that Luke believed it? Of course, it is proper, with Bishop Gore, to turn the argument around and say that Luke did teach it; therefore, Paul his master *must* have known it. But to many such a suggestion is unconvincing. It is far more likely that if the verses in question were written by Luke he was recording, after he separated from Paul, one of the many stories current in Palestine. He may have recognized that the traditions which he incorporated into the introduction to the Gospel, such as the genealogy and the story of the Birth, were inconsistent with each other. But it may not have troubled him at all. In other words, he may have followed the example of the compiler of the Old Testament, who has left us two accounts of the Creation, two of the Flood, and two of David's introduction to Saul, which contradict each other; but the compiler thought best to incorporate both into the narrative, as each had some significance. This may well have been the mind of Luke.

Is the conclusion, then, that there is no Scriptural evidence which gives ground for the belief that this doctrine expresses a historic fact?

Far from it. Those who are convinced that it is a historic fact find support in the record. But, on the other hand, it should be recognized that those who fail to find mention of it in any Apostolic writing in the New Testament; who think that it is contradicted by Paul and "John"; who find but two verses in Luke—and those in a part of the story which is of doubtful authority; who have learned that Matthew's story is based upon a mistranslation of the ancient text, ought not to be accused of prejudice if they state that their reading of the Holy Scriptures, with the aid of such studies as help to an understanding of the same, has led to the conclusion that the evidence does not justify them in stating that the Virgin Birth is a historic fact, but rather that it is a beautiful symbolic expression of the sublime and fundamental truth recorded in the Fourth Gospel of the spiritual birth of every child of God, and therefore supremely true of the Perfect Son of God—that he was born, not of blood nor of the will of man nor of the will of the flesh, but of God.

How the belief in the Virgin Birth, if it were not a historic fact, arose, we cannot tell. But having once arisen, as Harnack and other scholars believe, from a reading of prophecy as it came to the early Church in the Greek translation, it fell on fertile ground. Even those who deny that it arose in the Gentile world, recognize how congenial it was to Gentile thought. It is told of Buddha; among the Greeks every hero was believed to have had one human and one divine parent; and the "Mystery" religions, with their saviour-gods also miraculously born, were making a strong appeal to the imagination of the world when the Gospels passed into Asia Minor and Greece.

But apart from these, there were other elements at work. Even in St. Paul's Epistles we find evidence of the influence of the Manichean heresy which taught that matter is essentially evil, and that therefore the holy life was to be identified with the ascetic life. St. Paul, although he recognized the disciplinary value of asceticism, nevertheless vehemently protested against an asceticism based upon belief that matter is essentially evil; and the account of Jesus' life as one who "went about eating and drinking, the friend of publicans and sinners," shows how far the primitive Gospel was from the Manichean heresy. But that Oriental thought made a strong appeal to men of old, as it does to-day, and the Church deviated more and more from the early belief.

In the early Church, marriage was considered "an honorable estate, instituted of God in the time of man's innocency, signifying unto us the mystical union that is betwixt Christ and his Church." But when the Church, passing from that earlier period which had glorified marriage, coming into a corrupt society such as is described by Juvenal, degraded by the lust of the flesh, came to feel that virginity was a higher state than matrimony, believers could not without sacrilege express their faith as we believe Paul and "John" and Mark and Peter expressed it. Although not one word from the pure lips of Mary, save possibly one verse in Luke, nor from the divine lips of Jesus could be found to justify this explanation of the Incarnation; although several sayings of both seem to contradict it, nevertheless the early Church could express its faith in no other way. It was obliged to say that He was born of a Virgin, because otherwise men would have felt that something less than the glory of human life was attributed to him. Now, those who do not so think; those who have outgrown the awful doctrine of Augustine of Original Sin—that every child born into this world is corrupt because it is the fruit of the union of a man with a woman; those who do not think that a physical miracle adds to the glory of a "supernatural" Person, turn to the Scriptures and ask if they cannot be delivered from a primitive conception of the universe, of man, of God recorded in the Church's history; and yet be saved by faith in Jesus.[17]

But the Traditionalists are not entirely at one. There is both a Right and a Left wing. It is the "Protestant" wing which, accepting this doctrine of the Virgin Birth, denies that Mary continued a virgin after the birth of Jesus. They read in the Gospels that Mary and Joseph lived apparently as husband and wife for certainly twelve years after the birth of Mary's first-born. But they repudiate the notion that this was a simulacrum of marriage. Yet there can be no question that the Perpetual Virginity of the Blessed Virgin is a fundamental element in the Catholic tradition, and this is accepted by the "Catholic" Traditionalists. They believe that virginity is a higher form of life than can be found in marriage and many of them prove their faith by their works. The final and, as it seems to some of us, the inevitable step was taken by the Roman Catholic Church which asserted that not only was our Saviour born of a virgin but that that Virgin herself must have been Immaculately Conceived, as otherwise the taint might have descended to her Son. The dogma of the Immaculate Conception is modern in its formal statement* but it represents the flower of the Catholic tradition. The sceptic may well ask if the Immaculate Conception of the Blessed Virgin does not lead to the immaculate conception of Saint Anne and so on, back to Seth, the son of Adam?

Now, as I understand it, the Modernist does not feel himself bound by this tradition, either by that part of it which the "Anglo-Catholic" accepts or by its beginning, which is congenial to the thought of the "Protestant" Traditionalist. In other words, he believes that he has returned to the earliest tradition of the Church before the doctrine of the Virgin Birth had been suggested. And this conclusion is one which the Modernist believes the scholarly Traditionalists will ultimately adopt. He finds confirmation

* 1854.

for that expectation in the sane words of Bishop Gore, who, while he firmly believes in the Virgin Birth as a historic fact and is confident that the testimony of the Scriptures is sufficient for that belief, nevertheless, as a careful scholar, states his position in the present controversy in words which the Modernist believes conclusive:* "Nothing concerning His birth—except His descent from David, which was apparently undisputed, and that He belonged to the family of Joseph, the carpenter of Nazareth, who apparently died before the public ministry began, and of Mary, who certainly survived into the early days of the Church—entered into the first preaching of the gospel or the first *knowledge*" (italics mine) "of the Church. Certainly nothing concerning the birth of Christ was part of that assurance on the basis of which faith in Jesus was claimed. I may add that it ought not to this day to form part of the basis of the claim."[18]

* Bishop Gore, in a recent letter, has called attention to another statement on this question in a later book, "Belief in Christ." His letter, together with quotations from both books, will be found in *The Churchman* of February 16, 1924. The essential point is that this accurate scholar, believing in the Virgin Birth as a historic fact, concedes that "the question of the birth" (I assume he means manner of birth) "is secondary, not primary."

And now we come to the consideration of the ethical justification of the Modernist, for the Traditionalist may say: "Even if it be admitted that the Modernist's theory is true, the conclusion must be that every man who believes it to be true is debarred by the Truth from reciting the Creed, which on his theory must be false."

CHAPTER IV

INTELLECTUAL INTEGRITY

There are few things of which the average Protestant is more suspicious than of casuistry, and rightly so, for he knows something of its history: it has led to moral confusion and has been a terrible instrument in enslaving simple folk and establishing priestcraft. When, then, a man even seems to hesitate when asked to answer what appears to be a plain question concerning right and wrong, the conclusion seems to be that he must be lacking either in intelligence or integrity.

When, then, the Traditionalist asserts that every intelligent and honest man is under an obligation to "say what he means and to mean what he says," he looks at the Modernist and demands that he should answer the challenge without delay. Nevertheless I shall ask that judgment be suspended till this dictum be examined. As the statement of a general principle it is not only true but a truism, that is, it needs no emphasis, for it is accepted by all intelligent and honest men. But when it is proposed to use it as a touchstone in a controversy in which passions are excited, intricate questions of history are to be examined, and metaphysical problems are involved, the Modernist is obliged to ask, not what the general question means, but what application it has in the present controversy.

If the dictum be reduced to a syllogism, the problem will be clearly apprehended. "All intelligent and honest men are under an obligation to say what they mean and mean what they say. The Modernist does not say plainly what he means or does not mean explicitly what he says. *Ergo* he must be lacking either in intelligence or integrity."

Let us consider first the conclusion: "What is meant by the Modernist? Is he a fiction of a heated imagination or is he a man whom we know, whose intelligence we can test by what he says or writes?" I know a good many Modernists and I do not think that an unprejudiced man would say that the average Modernist is less intelligent than the average Traditionalist. Possibly the Traditionalist would say that the

Modernist is more intelligent than the Fundamentalist.

Then he must be lacking in integrity. That is a wide-spread belief. Yet if, again, we turn from the imaginary Modernist to consider the lives of those who hold Modernist opinions, the old proverb "*falsus in uno falsus in omnibus*" seems to be proved unsound. Do the Modernists appear to be irreverent in the services of the Church? Do they fail to visit the "widows and fatherless" in their affliction? Are they more "spotted by the world" than their more orthodox brethren? There can be but one answer to these questions. Therefore those who are suspicious of the Modernist must take the step which Jesus insisted upon when the same accusation was brought against him. "Either make the tree good, and his fruit good; or else make the tree corrupt, and his fruit corrupt: for the tree is known by his fruit. . . . A good man out of the good treasures of the heart bringeth forth good things: and an evil man out of the evil treasures bringeth forth evil things" (Matthew 12:33 and 35).

As the business man, to whom this dictum is supposed to make a special appeal, is expected to say: "Let us get down to cases." I will say nothing of the hundreds of earnest, devout, self-denying, studious men now living who are known in the communities in which they live and are honored of all good men; I will only ask if such suspicion can attach to those who have died in the faith—Alexander V. G. Allen, Harry Nash, Cyril W. Emmet, Dean Rashdall? Were those men lacking in intelligence or integrity? If in the first, they were more foolish than most of us, for they fasted and prayed and labored more abundantly than all of us, and yet at the end had nothing to show for their pains. The second question I will not even ask, for the mere asking of it would be the condemnation of those who would be driven to say: "They cast out devils through Beelzebub, the chief of the devils." And we have our Saviour's word that that leads to the sin against the Holy Ghost. Who, then, is the Modernist who is supposed to be condemned by this formula? I answer that he is a figment of an excited imagination.

If the Traditionalist is prepared to say that he believes that his Modernist brother is a hypocrite—an actor, playing a part for the wage that is paid him; that, in the trenchant words which

Horace Greeley sometimes used of a political opponent, "He lies and he knows that he lies," then the Modernist is content to be silent and leave the question to the common sense of good men and women whose judgments have not been paralyzed by passion—to "Him Who knoweth the secrets of the heart." But there are not many who are willing publicly to denounce their brethren as hypocrites; that is, who in this, say plainly what they mean or mean what they say.

Let us now examine the major premise: "A man must say what he means and mean what he says." The first clause is an intellectual demand, and the assumption is that any intelligent man can meet it without hesitation. Macaulay once boasted that he had never written a sentence which could be misunderstood by an intelligent man; but how many of us can make such a boast? We are trying to say what we mean, but we do not always succeed. It can be done when we are dealing with simple matters, such as mathematics, where there is no doubt as to the meaning of the terms used. To say that two plus two equals four is to say exactly what one means, because the speaker knows that the words he uses will convey exactly the same meaning to the hearer as is in his own mind. The same is true of a legal document, where the two parties to a contract are supposed to be agreed upon the meaning of the terms used and the obligations arising from the agreement. But when we are dealing with what are called Universals, there is no such agreement. Truth, Beauty, Goodness, God are concepts which cannot be defined. It is not possible for any man to say of such ideas exactly what he means, first because words are incapable of expressing the "deep things of the Spirit"; and second because it is impossible to know how the words spoken by one man will be interpreted by another. Phillips Brooks, who was not lacking in intelligence (though some of the orthodox in his day believed him to be dishonest), was once asked if he believed in God, and replied that he could not answer categorically yes or no. It is often impossible for a man to say plainly what he means.

But there is another reason for this inability to state plainly what one means. It is not due to the speaker but to the hearer. The hearer may have a very simple idea of an exceedingly complex question, and any attempt on the part of the speaker to make plain what *he* understands, may seem to the hearer either unintelligible or disingenuous.

Now consider the second clause: he must "mean what he says." Let us apply that to the article of the Creed which is the storm centre of the present controversy—the Virgin Birth. I believe that much of the bitterness of spirit would be sweetened if both Fundamentalist and Traditionalist understood clearly what the position of the Modernist is in this matter. The Traditionalist says, "Here is a plain statement of a 'fact,' that is, a physical miracle. The words were clearly understood by the men who spoke them to mean that Jesus was born without the agency of a human father. Some of the Modernists believe that Joseph was his father. How then can an intelligent and honest man use words which express belief in a fact when he denies the fact? He does not mean what he says."

But attention has already been called to the fact that many Modernists believe as the Traditionalist does in this matter. Their contention is that the emphasis is laid upon this article as if the men who first used the words were chiefly interested in the physical miracle, of which I shall have a word to say later. There are Modernists who do not believe the physical miracle which the words unquestionably express. But I never heard of any Modernist who questioned that when this expression was incorporated into the Apostles' Creed, the Church doubted that the words meant what they clearly do mean. I know of no Modernist who has fallen into the error of Origen and Augustine, of interpreting ancient words allegorically so as to give them a modern meaning. They have studied history and recognize that there has been an evolution of thought: first that which is "natural"—physical, and afterward that which is "spiritual." The Modernist's contention is that he is applying the method of spiritualizing the statement of a physical fact in this article of the Creed which the Traditionalist has applied to other articles of the Creed.

For example, "Creation" is conceived in the Creeds as a physical fact which took place at a given time and in the way described in the book of Genesis. The Fundamentalist interprets that exactly as it was understood by the men of old; but the Traditionalist does not. He knows that in the second century no other conception was possible but now there is a more majestic thought of God, the Creating Life. The Traditionalist knows more about history than does the Fundamentalist. He knows that what the makers of the Creed wished to express was (in opposition to the Gnostics) not a cosmic fact but the truth that all things visible and invisible were brought to light, not by a malign or impure god, but by the Father revealed in Jesus Christ.

He knows that the "descent into hell" was originally conceived as a miracle which occurred at a definite time in a definite place. He has a different opinion, yet desires to retain the ancient faith, even though he be not clear as to what the obscure words "went into the place of departed spirits" exactly mean. But he knows that the reason those words were put into the Creed was not to emphasize the conception of the universe which Dante later immortalized in Hell and Purgatory and Paradise, but to emphasize the reality of Jesus' death, which men found it so hard to believe of one whom they had now come to speak of as "God of God."

The Traditionalist knows that when the Ascension is spoken of, it meant a physical miracle, a body lifted from the Mount of Olives to some point in space beyond the stars, which were not far above the earth. The science of astronomy has made it impossible for him to retain the ancient thought; he knows that if the body of Jesus had begun to ascend from the Mount of Olives nineteen hundred years ago it would not to-day, even with the velocity of light, have reached the farthest stars revealed by the telescope. In other words, in order to mean by these words what was originally meant, it would be necessary to abandon the heliocentric theory of the universe and return to the primitive geocentric theory. But he repeats the ancient words because he knows that the men of old who used these words were not interested in astronomical fact but in the faith that he who had been crucified and buried and rose again, "God had exalted with power," and therefore He had power to exalt the faithful so that "with Him they might continually dwell."

In regard to these supposed "facts" the Traditionalist has used the liberty of interpretation which has been characteristic of the Church from earliest ages. Is he, then, to be accused of insincerity when he uses an ancient formula to express a thought which the exact language employed may seem to debar?

Therefore, the Modernist, when he is accused of imbecility or disingenuousness in the use of words whose intellectual connotation he repudiates, is tempted to say to the Traditionalist what the Colonial governor of Rhode Island wrote to Governor Winthrop of Connecticut: "You may assure yourselves that if wee split you will sinke; for wee are both upon one bottom and I am apte to conclude as many rents and leaks on your part as on ours if not some trunnel holes open." [1]

This truth has, I think, been overlooked by the Traditionalists. For example, Bishop Manning, in his "A Message to the Diocese," which is a dignified and impressive statement and breathes a spirit of fairness which might with advantage be imitated by some of his Episcopal brethren, calls in twenty-seven Unitarian ministers as impartial witnesses to show what disinterested men think of the Modernists' position. "'With all courtesy and considerateness let us make it plain that religious teachers who play with words in the most solemn relations of life, *who make their creeds mean what they were not originally intended to mean*'" (italics mine), "'or mentally reject a formula of belief while outwardly repeating it, cannot expect to retain the allegiance of men who are accustomed to straight thinking and square dealing.'"[2] I fear that these willing witnesses may, under cross examination, be found to prove more than the Traditionalist desires. It is not alone the Modernist whom the Unitarian condemns. It is the Traditionalist as well. According to the Unitarian, any man who uses the creeds as meaning "what they were not originally intended to mean . . . cannot expect to retain the allegiance of men who are accustomed to straight thinking and square dealing."

Not to analyze the Creed again, take but one article: "I believe in the resurrection of the body." There is no doubt what those words "originally meant"—they meant that the "flesh" (that was the word, not "body" which we interpret "spiritual body") would come out of the grave at the last day. There are many devout Christians, probably the vast majority, who believe as the early Christians did, in the "fact." The Unitarian does not, and therefore will not say the Creed. The Traditionalist repeats the Creed. Does he believe in the "fact"? There is great confusion of thought about "facts." A fact is something tested by the senses or by the intellect, not an object of faith. There are facts asserted in the Creed which are learned as other facts of history have been learned. There are other things stated as "facts" which are matters of faith or hope. The fact may be doubted yet the faith and hope which it symbolized may remain unshaken. Creation, descent into hell, ascension, and the resurrection of the body were originally conceived as "facts." No educated man to-day believes them to be facts, but symbols of truth. How much controversy might have been saved if, instead of insisting that the man who recites the Creed must be asserting his acceptance of "*facts*," it were recognized that he is expressing his belief in *truth*. Which are facts and which are matters of faith is the question between the Modernist and the Traditionalist. Both are condemned by the Unitarian. Only the Fundamentalist, whom the Unitarian would identify with the ignorant, can use the Creed in a way that meets his approval. The witness proves too much!

But reflection might lead our twenty-seven Unitarian brethren to consider whether they also do not fall under the same condemnation as those who use the historic Creeds with either much or little freedom. They also have a Creed; they believe and assert their belief that "the Lord our God is One." They take that Creed from an ancient writing. Do they mean by the word "God" what those who first used it meant? Did Moses, Isaiah, and Jesus use it as expressing the same exact idea as the modern Unitarian has? Can any word express what the religious soul means by the Divine? Do they say what they mean and mean what they say when they use the word "God"? Certainly they do, but only by escaping from the letter of their own dogmatism.

I am told that when a distinguished Unitarian, whom I am not at liberty to name, read Bishop Lawrence's book, "Fifty Years," he told a friend that he had intended to write to Bishop Lawrence, asking how, with the views expressed in that book, he could continue to say the Creed. "But," he added, "on reflection I was led to ask myself if I was justified in the daily use of the Lord's Prayer: 'Our Father who art in heaven' —*in heaven?* Do I mean by that exactly what Jesus meant? So I decided not to write to Bishop Lawrence."

I have dwelt at some length upon this, because I am told that this dictum, "A man must say what he means and mean what he says," has now become a sort of magic touchstone by which heresy can be detected. But I fear that it may be found that some of those who glibly use this phrase have fallen into the error which they condemn. No doubt the scholarly Traditionalist has been mortified by the efforts of zealous men who have attempted to come to the "help of the Lord" and have written to the newspapers stating that any clergyman who denies the "Immaculate Conception" is violating his ordination vow to teach the doctrine of the Church of which he is a minister. Had such a man, before mailing his letter to the newspaper, taken the trouble to consult the Irish Catholic policeman on the corner, he might have learned from him that the "Immaculate Conception" refers to the birth of the Mother of God, who was brought into the world without the taint of original sin, and has nothing to do with the Incarnation of Jesus Christ. Such a man, no doubt, was trying to say what he meant, but failed. He did not mean what he said, but it does not follow from this that he is either imbecile or dishonest. It only means that he is ignorant. Why not give the Modernist a chance to escape by the path of ignorance? Then the duty of the Church would be plain enough, to convince him by an appeal to the Scriptures or by reason (of which Hooker says one is as good a guide as the other),[3] instead of vilifying him and sowing the seeds of suspicion which cannot fail to produce the fruits of the flesh.

The truth is, that all the American Protestant churches are more or less influenced by that conception of a creed which prevailed in New England in colonial days. Each new township was a swarm from an older Congregation and set forth a creed to which each settler subscribed. It was a legal document which each voter, who had to be a church member, signed. The creed was the charter by which he was bound both as a church member and a citizen. Every jot and tittle of it was binding. Sometimes these creeds were enrolled as part of the law.[4] The subscription to such a creed was as binding as every legal document is. If any man later became dissatisfied, he was at liberty to go out into the wilderness and start a new settlement with a new creed. It would seem strange that some of those who most loudly deplore the "dissidence of dissent" and are most strenuous in the cause of Church unity, should now be offering the same liberty to their brethren who do not interpret an ancient creed as they do. But it is not as strange as it seems, because they hold the old Puritan view of a creed as a legal document, and ignore the history of the formation of the Catholic Creeds.

But if we turn to the Apostles' Creed, we find that it was not originally set forth formally by the Church. It was a slow evolution.[5] Probably its *foundation* is to be found in the confession of faith made by the catechumen at baptism—faith in God as Father, Son, and Holy Spirit. The original confession as seen in the Acts of the Apostles was belief in Jesus as the Messiah. But when the Church passed out of the Jewish into the Gentile atmosphere, the primitive creed was found insufficient. There had been a great spiritual experience, and in the communion of the soul with God it had come to be recognized that St. Paul's statement that "by Christ we have access through one Spirit unto the Father" expressed not a metaphysical doctrine of the Being of God but the spiritual experience of souls in communion with God.

When, however, the simple-minded Christians began to be perplexed by the theories of those who were known as Gnostics, teaching that the Father, into Whose presence the soul had been brought by Christ, was not the Creator; that creation implied contact with matter which is essentially evil, the teachers of the Church taught the catechumens that the Father, to whom Christ had brought them, was the Creator not only of heaven but also of the earth on which they lived. And when other theories began to perplex the believer and men who were known as Docetists, influenced by the old Manichean theory, emphasized the essential corruption of matter, and consequently denied that Jesus had ever had a human body but only appeared to have such a body, the pastors told the people that any man "who denied that Jesus Christ had come in the flesh" was not speaking the truth of God; that Jesus really was born, suffered, and died. And standing upon this fundamental doctrine in which they found a living truth which enabled them to endure the common experiences of life, by which they could follow the footsteps of our Lord, even to martyrdom, they expanded their Creed into those articles which, beginning with the birth and ending with the death, laid emphasis upon the reality of Jesus' human nature.

Now, unless this truth be recognized, it will be supposed that the object of the teachers of the Church was to lay emphasis by the enlarged Creed upon the Divinity of Jesus, because that is what many men deny to-day. But in the second century, the Divinity of Jesus gave no trouble. It was his Humanity which was the stumbling block, and in order to impress upon the people the historic reality of the Man Christ Jesus, the name of his mother was given and the name of the governor under whom he was put to death. But when they named his mother, they named her in accordance with the prevailing opinion, which believed that she was a virgin at the time of his birth and that he had no human father. But to suppose that in the formation of the Creed it was the virginity of the mother upon which emphasis was laid is to misread the whole history. It was the reality of his birth which the Creed emphasized, and the manner of his birth was not even discussed. It was taken for granted that the tradition which was then prevalent was not only true but the only tradition.

The expansion of the third revelation of God as Spirit was not formulated as we now have it in the Creed until centuries later, though it is seen that the earliest step was taken in the declaration which appears in the first form of the Creed, that by the Spirit Jesus had been raised from the dead and therefore would quicken our mortal bodies by the Spirit that dwelleth in us; that he had been lifted to the right hand of God and would come in glory to judge the world.

The Fundamentalist repeats every article of the Creed *ex animo*,* because he is intellectually still in the second century. The Traditionalist repeats the same Creed also *ex animo* but, having passed out of the intellectual atmosphere of the second century, interprets certain articles in accordance with the intellectual change which he has experienced. The Modernist also re-

* That is, with a clear conscience.

peats the ancient words *ex animo* but interprets every article in accordance with the intellectual atmosphere which he is breathing. If the test is to be intellectual agreement with the opinions of the men who first uttered these words, it is a question whether any educated man to-day is justified in repeating the Creed. But if it once be admitted that the repetition of the Creed is not an assertion of agreement with *opinions* but the declaration of *faith*, then the Modernist believes that he is saying what he means, because he is using words to express his faith, which he believes to be identical with the faith once delivered to the saints. He means what he says, but it is faith he means.

This may not be clear to the casual reader, because the word "faith" like the word "sight" is used in two different senses. We speak of a man having good sight, meaning that his optic nerve reacts normally to light. We also speak of a beautiful or ugly sight, meaning an object which the eye perceives. In the same way we speak of "faith" meaning a spiritual activity, as when it is said, "Abraham believed God." But we also speak of "faith" as the formulation of a spiritual experience. But inasmuch as that formulation must be made in human language and in accordance with the intellectual presuppositions of the day in which it is uttered, faith is often supposed to be identical with those intellectual conceptions. But as a matter of fact it should be identified with the truth or spiritual reality, which no intellectual conception can adequately express. When, then, it is said that a man's faith to-day is the same as the faith of a man who lived in the fourth century, it is untrue if "faith" be identified with intellectual conceptions, but it is true if by "faith" we mean the truth which was the result of spiritual experience and which spiritual experience to-day recognizes and repeats.

As long as the Creed is supposed to be a catalogue of "facts" all that is required is intellectual assent, which means that the mind of the modern man must return to the intellectual conditions of the early Church. But if the Creed means to express faith in God the Creator, in Christ the Redeemer, and in the Holy Spirit the Sanctifier, then the Church to-day may, with a clear conscience, repeat the noble language which it has inherited, to testify that it holds that truth of God to which the ancient Church bore witness.

We have been speaking of the Apostles' Creed, but the principle of interpretation maintained is more clearly seen when we come to the consideration of what is called the "Nicene" Creed. The demand that a man "must say what he means" is legitimate when he expresses himself in language for which he alone is responsible. But it is not legitimate when applied to an ancient document for which he is not responsible. For example, it is possible to impale a man on one horn of the dilemma—imbecility or dishonesty—when he begins the service with the declaration "from the rising of the sun unto the going down of the same." But this is not done because a modern congregation understands that the words do not "mean what they say." Certainly they do not say what the congregation means. Yet they are used with a clear conscience because, though the "fact" which they express is denied by intelligent men and women to-day, the thought of the Omnipresence of God the congregation is glad to express in the noble language of the men of old.

Have the words of the Nicene Creed a greater sanctity than those of the Scriptures? I suspect that if the question were probed, it would be found that some of the Traditionalists would confess that they have. But if we re-read the sober words of the Twenty-first of the Thirty-nine Articles of the English Church (a fine example of the "irresistible force of understatement"), "General Councils . . . (forasmuch as they be an assembly of men whereof all be not governed by the Spirit and Word of God) may err and sometimes have erred," we shall not be justified in ascribing such sanctity to the Nicene Creed. If we study the history of the Council and consider the forces at work, we may be led to the conclusion that the Creed was of the nature of a compromise. Probably no one of the bishops present at that Council was entirely satisfied with every statement. We know that some who were present would not accept it; that others accepted it reluctantly; that after the Council had adjourned, there were disputes as to the meaning of the Creed, and that the disputes continued for over a hundred years, until at last the Church sought to end the discussion by calling in the strong arm of the Empire to drive into exile all who called a single word in question.

If any one should be shocked by being told that the Council of Nicaea was more like a political convention assembled in the midst of a heated presidential campaign, and that the Creed was not unlike the "party platform" with which no one is quite satisfied, but which on the whole does express the party faith, let him read the history of the Council,[6] and he will find food for thought. The history of the dissensions in the Council is not pleasant reading, nor do they express the whole truth. There is another side to the story. The men who gathered at that Council were, many of them, devout Christians, and they did attempt to set forth what they believed to be the truth about the Eternal Son of God. They probably did this as well as it could be done in the prevailing metaphysical, political, ecclesiastical, social, and moral atmosphere of their time. The faith is expressed in the metaphysical language of the day. Certainly, if the Creed were written today, we should use different language. When we repeat it, we cannot be sure that we mean what they meant. Why, then, do we repeat it? Because our faith is the same as theirs: that the Son's Divinity was not different from, nor merely "like," but essentially the *same* as the Divinity of the Father. We are glad to use the ancient words that we may testify that our faith is the same as that of the Church in the fourth century. But if we go beyond that we shall be involved in many difficulties. As a matter of fact, the Creed was not originally intended to be used in public worship; it was simply a statement of what the majority of the bishops could be induced to sign.

Now, it cannot be denied that the letter of the article of the Creed which speaks of the birth of Christ from a virgin does express what was believed to be a fact and that some of the Modernists deny the fact; and if the fact be the vital element, the Modernist has no standing. But if the faith be the essential element, then the Modernist who denies the fact believes himself justified in using the ancient formula as the expression of his living faith. And this conclusion he reaches, not alone by the exercise of private judgment; he believes that he is justified by the history of the Church and by the teaching of the Prayer Book. For he notes first that in the Creeds set forth by the Council of Nicaea, emphasis is laid upon the reality of Jesus' birth, but there is no mention of the virginity of Mary. He does not suggest that this was omitted because there was any doubt in the minds of the bishops as to the fact, but he does conclude that they could not have felt that that fact was an essential element of the faith.

He also knows that it was not until the fifth century that the Nicene Creed (as modified by the Councils of Constantinople and Chalcedon, in direct opposition to the anathema pronounced by Nicaea upon those who should alter that Creed) was introduced into the liturgy of the Church. "The Catholic Church existed for four centuries, at its best and doing its greatest work, without any creed in its office, liturgical or other. . . . The Creed was first introduced into the liturgy about 470. . . . The Creed was neither sung nor said during mass at Rome until the time of Benedict VIII (1012–1024)." [7] Therefore the Modernist believes that this insistence upon the letter of the Creed as a test of faith is unjustified by the history of the Church.

I think it is not too much to say that if faith was to be tested by the literal acceptance of the original meaning attached to the various statements in the Catholic Creeds, the English Church at the Reformation would never have incorporated them into its liturgy. For it is to be remembered that the English Church was originally the religious expression of the English nation, and that the English conception of law underlay the English Church's conception of ancient formularies. The Latin, particularly the French, mind is essentially logical and prefers to formulate the law in a code where each imaginable infringement is provided for by a clear statement limiting the rights of the individual. But the English conception is entirely different. The common law presupposes certain fundamental principles, and these principles are applied to each case in dispute as it is brought before the court. The court then decides whether the underlying principle which an ancient formula contains applies to the case in question. The problem is not whether the letter of an ancient law decides the point in dispute, but whether the letter permits an interpretation which brings the principle into relation with a new experience. This is what Tennyson calls "broadening down from precedent to precedent." The French method may be the better one, but the English mind, which is not logical but pragmatic, has always preferred to follow the method of the common law—freedom from the letter, by an interpretation of the spirit or intention. The Puritan, with all his fine moral qualities, did not represent the mind of England, either politically or ecclesiastically, but, so far as I know, attention has never been called to the fact that the Puritan was profoundly influenced by that great French logician, Calvin. Therefore, to the Puritan, a creed is a code. To the English Church, the Creed was an ancient formula which was to be interpreted in accordance with the experiences arising in a new day. Therefore, in the English Church there has always been allowed wide liberty of interpretation. The formula of the Anglo-Catholic, heard some thirty years ago, that "fixity of interpretation is of the essence of the creed" is not English. It is Latin; it is Puritan. "The fact that theological thought follows the evolution which governs all other thought, that it changes from age to age, largely as regards the relative emphasis given to its various elements, not inconsiderably as regards these elements themselves, is a fact written largely across the pages of ecclesiastical history. . . . No agreement about theological or any other doctrine insures or indeed is capable of producing a sameness of belief."[8] The same principle has influenced American history.[9]

When, then, the Modernist turns to the authoritative teaching of the Church of which he is a member, he finds that while every child must be taught the Creed, when the child is asked what he "chiefly" learns, that is, what is the essential element in the Creed, the answer is: Belief in God the Father, who hath made him, and all the world; the Son who hath redeemed him, and all mankind; the Holy Spirit who sanctifieth him, and all the people of God.* In other words, he finds that according to the teaching of the Church of which he is a member, the essential element in this Creed is the one that had been emphasized by St. Paul long before any Creed had been formulated—that the soul of the child should look forward to being brought by Christ through the Spirit into the very presence of God the Father.

Now turn to a consideration of the requirements of the Church of England for the clergy. We have become so familiar with the Anglo-Catholic's disparagement of the Reformation and so complacent in his attempts to revolution-

* See Prayer Book, p. 267.

ize the services of the Church, that both clergy and laity alike have forgotten how radical was the action of the English Church in abandoning the Roman Ordinal and substituting our present offices of ordination. In the Roman Church, priest and bishop are examined carefully in regard to each article of the Nicene Creed. But in the English Church all this has been omitted, and the candidate for ordination is asked if he believes the Holy Scriptures to be the Word of God; if he is determined to preach nothing as necessary to salvation but what he shall be persuaded can be proved by these Scriptures; and whether he will teach the doctrine "as this Church hath received the same." What doctrine? A different doctrine from that which his sponsors in baptism promised that he should be taught? Is he asked whether he will teach all the "doctrines" which from time to time may be insisted upon by those who call themselves orthodox? No such question is asked. He is asked whether he will preach the doctrine, and that doctrine is: faith in God as Father, Son, and Holy Spirit. It is the Apostles' Creed which is still the test of bishop, priest, and deacon, as of layman.

The opinion that the very letter of the Creed is binding upon the consciences of men and that those who use the Creed except in its original significance are anarchists, has led to the troubling of many devout souls. They have come to believe that the doctrine of the Virgin Birth expresses a stupendous miracle, and are in danger of resting upon that, forgetting that its value is a spiritual one. They fear that if it be called in question, then there is no assurance that Jesus is without the taint of sin; that there is no authority for declaring him to be Unique—in other words, that he is only a little better than the best of men; and above all, that the denial of the fact is equivalent to denial of faith in the Divinity of the Saviour.

This review of history may seem to some a digression, even an attempt to escape from a definite answer to the question with which it began. But its purpose has been to lead men to consider whether, when the demand is made that a man should say what he means and mean what he says, the intention is not really to insist that he should state plainly what he *does not mean.* In other words, it is not a demand for the assertion of a positive faith, but for the expression of a negative opinion so phrased that it may give ground for an ecclesiastical trial. In other words, it is an attempt to "entangle men in their talk" in order to accuse them. When the Modernist fails—following the example of his Master—to answer certain questions in the way that the opponent desires, it is supposed that he is actuated by some sinister motive. But the spirit of charity might lead to the conclusion that the Modernist desires to avoid the scandal of a trial for heresy, not because of any personal inconvenience, but because he is convinced that it would be detrimental to the life of the whole Church, and that if the "heresy hunt" once begins, it cannot end where the Traditionalist or the Fundamentalist would desire.

If, then, the Modernist be asked why, if he does not believe the fact, he does not say plainly that he does not believe it, his answer may be (if he be a clergyman) that he has a deep sense of responsibility. He knows that however much emphasis may be laid upon private judgment, there is to be found in every congregation a considerable number of people who are trusting the authority of the teacher and taking their opinions from him. If, then, he were to say plainly that he does not believe the Virgin Birth to be a historic fact, he might easily shatter the faith of those who are trusting the Divine Saviour. One would think that this would meet with the approval of serious-minded men, instead of being made a reproach. But when the Modernist is asked if he feels justified in using words which literally express a historic fact, when he no longer believes that fact, he answers that he means, when he uses the words, not to express a historic fact but to emphasize his faith in and loyalty to Jesus Christ, the Incarnate Son of God. To him virginity means purity. To the men of old, purity was so associated automatically with virginity that virginity was accepted without questioning. He believes their opinions to have been a mistake, but his faith is the same as theirs—faith in the sinlessness of Jesus Christ; that whatever may have been the physical means by which the body of Jesus was brought into this world, it is true of Him as it is not true of any, that He was born "not of blood nor of the will of the flesh nor of the will of man, but of God." He believes that in using the ancient words in a sense different from that of the men of old in regard to the new Creation, he is doing exactly what every educated man is doing when he uses the ancient words in regard to the first Creation. He believes that God is the Background, the Source, the ever-present Cause of life, but he has long abandoned the opinion of "Creation" in the sense in which the men of old understood that word. He uses the ancient words to express his belief in the uniqueness of Jesus, but to him that uniqueness is revealed, not by any physical miracle but by the supreme supernatural character revealed in the words, the deeds, the mighty spiritual experiences, the unique consciousness, and the perpetual influence of the living Christ in the world to-day. He uses the ancient words to express his faith in the divinity of Jesus Christ. He does not believe that that divinity is dependent upon any physical miracle (he finds that many of the Traditionalists do not believe it). He finds the evidences for that divinity in Jesus' unique consciousness of a relationship to God such as no other merely human being has ever attained to. He finds it manifested in the influence which Jesus produced upon the lives of the faithful men and women who followed him centuries ago, in the Life which transfigured the saints and glorified the humblest souls, in the influence which he experiences even in a slight degree of the presence of the living Christ to-day. He does not pretend that if he were writing a creed to-day he would use the phraseology of neo-Platonism. He is not sure what *ousia* and *hypostasis* and *homoiousios* exactly mean. He does not deny that it may have been necessary to attempt to define the faith in philosophic terms, and is glad to join in singing or saying the great confession of Nicaea as an outward and visible sign that he believes himself to be one in faith with those who in their day and generation declared in philosophic language their conviction of the essential divinity of our Lord.

But when he is examined in regard to his opinions, he prefers the language of St. Paul: "In him dwelt all the fullness of the Godhead bodily." When it is insisted that that must mean that the Omnipotence, the Omnipresence, and the Omniscience of the Transcendent God were revealed in human life, he frankly states that he not only finds no evidence of it in the Scriptures but that it is an incomprehensible thought. He does not think that those metaphysical terms are the best expression of what the soul has learned of God. He believes that the Scriptures provide us with better language: God is Love, God is Light, and God is Life. Love and Light and Life are supremely revealed in Jesus Christ. When those who seek to "entangle" the Modernist in his talk, insist that he should answer whether he believes that this divinity of Christ differs from the divinity of all good men in kind or in degree, he frankly states he does not know. Does the questioner know? He recognizes that he is far removed intellectually from Shakespeare and spiritually from Paul, but he knows that the distance which separates him from the dramatic genius of the one and the spiritual genius of the other is but a hand's breadth compared with the distance that separates the holiest saint from Jesus Christ, and, therefore, the difference may be so great in degree as to be equivalent to a difference in kind. But what is the value of all these subtle questionings? The essential thing is life. He believes that Jesus came to give life and give it abundantly. There are many things about Jesus which he may not believe, but he believes Jesus.

The mystic words of Luther show a deeper understanding of the spiritual significance of the doctrine of the Virgin Birth than many of the metaphysical formulas: "Every Christian may exult and boast in the birth of Jesus, just as though he himself had been physically born of Mary like Christ. Whoso doth not believe or doubteth this, is no Christian. This is the sense of Isaiah ix : 6, 'Unto us a Child is born, unto us a Son is given.' Us, us, to us it is born, to us it is given. Therefore see thou that thy delight in the Gospels is derived not solely from the history itself; for it exists not long: but make thou His birth thine own; exchange with Christ, so that thou mayest get quit of thy birth and appropriate His. This takes place when thou believest. Then wilt thou of a certainty lie in the womb of the Virgin Mary and be her dear child."[10]

Now, if the positive affirmations of the Modernist were recognized, the negative doubts or even denials would be seen to be of small consequence, unless the Church is prepared to say that the original meaning of every article of the Creed must be accepted *ex animo* by every believer. But no sensible man in the Episcopal

Church—whatever the Unitarians may say—holds any such opinion.

Now, to answer plainly the question, "Does the Modernist, when he repeats the words of the Creed, state plainly what he means?" His answer is that neither he nor the Traditionalist states exactly what it originally meant because they did not write the Creed, and that therefore the question is irrelevant. Moreover, the Modernist thinks that the form of the question is unworthy of churchmen. It seems to imply that he who is questioned must be discredited, whatever his reply may be. The Modernist recognizes that many good people are perplexed and seek to learn from him how he thinks the Creed can be used by men who have acquired the larger knowledge of the universe than had those who formulated the ancient articles of belief. In order to explain his position, the Modernist would suggest that the question be put in this form: First: "When you repeat the Creed do you mean what the men of old meant?" His answer is: "In many respects I do not, nor can any thoughtful man mean what the letter of the Creed implies." Second: "When you use the words of the Creed, what do you mean?"

He answers, "I mean to affirm that my faith in God—Father, Son, and Holy Spirit—is the same as the faith of the men of old, even when I am obliged to discard the opinions with which that faith has been long associated. I know that my brethren so use a part of the Creed in expressing their faith, and I believe I am justified in so using the whole of the Creed in expressing my faith in the truth contained in every article." This is neither unintelligent nor disingenuous. Whether it be *permissible* is a question which must be decided by the whole Church. Until it has been decided that this liberty of interpretation which has been characteristic of the English Church from the Reformation and of the Protestant Episcopal Church for over one hundred years must now be limited, the Modernist with a free conscience rejoices to recite the old formularies, and to bear witness to the unity of faith which is the same "yesterday, to-day, and forever," though the intellectual concepts involved in the ancient words change from age to age. But in the present form, the question seems to imply that the Modernist should mean what the Traditionalist means.

The Modernist deprecates in this discussion

the introduction of the question of integrity. He thinks that it should not "be mentioned among you as becometh saints." He has tried not to yield to the temptation to suspect his brother, however widely he differed from him, but if it be insisted that this question shall be introduced, then he will be compelled to ask that the test be applied to the Anglo-Catholic as well as to him. He will be obliged to ask how such men can remain as ministers of a church, the distinctive note of which from apostolic days has been progressive. If he be reactionary, he is not in sympathy with the church of which he is a member. If he holds office in a Protestant church and is attempting to eliminate the Protestant element, to make the clergy the directors of the consciences of the laity, to change the Holy Communion into the Mass, to "reserve the elements for adoration," then indeed the question of honesty is one that might profitably be pressed. But the Modernist is not inclined to do this, because he believes that those men who in his judgment are absolutely wrong, nevertheless believe themselves justified both by Scripture and by the standards of the church in doing that which they believe to be right, and recognizes that in spite of what he believes to be their error, they are ministering to souls who can be touched in no other way, and are opening to them treasures of spiritual value.

But if this larger liberty, based upon mutual trust, is to be replaced by the spirit of inquisition, the spirit of comprehension will no longer characterize the Protestant Episcopal Church. It has been the boast of the Episcopal Church that it was the most comprehensive church in America,[11] and that comprehension was based not upon a mere Latitudinarian toleration but upon mutual trust. If trust or faith in the intelligence and honesty of the clergy is shaken, the Episcopal Church will be compelled to abandon that position which differentiates it from other Protestant churches, and be compelled to choose between the individualism of the sect and the obedience of Roman Catholicism.

CHAPTER V

THE PURPOSE OF THE MODERNIST

I have been speaking of misunderstandings, but the fundamental misunderstanding is due to a misapprehension of the ultimate purpose of the Modernist. He is supposed to be a rationalist, unduly influenced by the dogmatism of modern science, and more interested in breaking down than in building up. But again, if instead of the imaginary Modernist, we test these opinions by the lives and works of the men we know, it will be found that this description is a caricature. I say nothing of the Episcopal Church, but consider who the men are in the Presbyterian, the Congregational, and the Baptist churches who are preaching the Word with power. The Modernist is less rationalistic and more mystic than is popularly supposed. He has been influenced by the scientific spirit, but he is far more influenced by the moral example of scientists than by their dogmatism. No man can read the life of Darwin without being profoundly impressed by the humility of the man, his willingness to acknowledge that long years of labor had led to a false conclusion: his soul was athirst for truth, the whole truth, and nothing but the truth; therefore, he was great in his humility, and ready to acknowledge his mistakes.

The Modernist finds that the ecclesiastical atmosphere has a tendency to exalt orthodoxy, ancient theories of truth, and to lead men to think that it is more important to be in accord with the popular teaching of the Church than to learn the truth which God is revealing to-day as truly as He revealed it of old. He is inspired by the example of the intellectual veracity of such a man as Huxley, and he finds that the obligation to repeat an ancient formula does raise very serious difficulties not only in his own mind but in the minds especially of the young, who in school and college are learning truths which are in conflict with the letter of the ancient formulas. He is trying to interpret the truth which the formulas attempt to express, in a way that can be accepted by truthful men who have gained a knowledge of which the ancient world was ignorant. He finds in the lives of many scientists an exhibition of that unconscious asceticism which does not seek poverty, hunger, and wearing toil in order to propitiate God, but accepts them because they are absorbed in the search for truth. There are many scientific students who are modern examples of the spirit of the early saints. He recognizes that such men as Agassiz and Pasteur were perfectly indifferent to the riches of the world, and unselfishly gave their lives for the benefit of mankind.[1] He knows that there are many physicians and nurses, quite unorthodox in their theory, who are doing the will of the Father in alleviating pain and curing the sick; that there are many lawyers who have abandoned even attendance at church worship, but are living to establish the reign of justice upon this earth; that there are men and women who have turned in bitterness against the Church, but are daily going about doing good, trying to lift men and women out of degrading, hopeless poverty into self-respect, that they may be efficient helpers in the upbuilding of civilization. He knows that there are many young men and women, pure in heart, loving truth, anxious to serve, to whom the Church makes no appeal.

If to those who are "at ease in Zion" the

Modernist seems to be destructive, it is because he is going after the lost sheep in the wilderness. It is not that he is indifferent to the inspiration which proceeds from the Reformation Confessions, the Catholic Creeds, the Visible Church, and even the Bible, but because he finds that the Church is tempted to make these things resting-places, instead of points of departure to the Promised Land; in other words, he is crying to the Church in the words of the prophetic writer of Deuteronomy, who saw in his day the same disposition to rest, "Ye have compassed this mountain long enough. Turn you northward"—towards the Promised Land. If this purpose of the Modernist were understood, it would be recognized that he is the true Fundamentalist. The Modernists are trying to reveal to the Church and to the world the true foundation on which the religion of Jesus and the Church of Christ rested at the beginning and rest to-day. They are Protestants, and yet they cannot fail to recognize that Protestant theology has fallen into disrepute. But they believe that to be due to a crystallization of Protestant dogma, a crystallization which prevents the truth from being a living principle in men's lives to-day. They ask themselves in wonder why it is that such words as "election" and "predestination," "reconciliation" and "justification," and "atonement," which once made men's hearts glow and gave them power and filled them with hope, should now fall cold and dead if they are even mentioned. They believe it is because men have lost an understanding of the living word and have substituted for it a dogma. The dogmatic statements which are identified with the Protestant Reformation no more reveal what those words meant to the men of the sixteenth century than a herbarium can reveal the glory of the rose and the fragrance of the lily and the shy beauty of the violet. The Modernists would call the Church back to a reconsideration of the foundation on which the dogmas rest, and they believe that if men could return to the words of Paul, they would find that these terms were not used to construct a scheme of salvation but to reveal the experience of the soul which had been saved by Christ.

To such a soul "election" meant that God loved him before he loved God; "predestination" meant the Father's preparation for the education of the child; "justification" was the acquittal of the sinner who came to God the Judge, led by Jesus Christ, and found that when he came before Him "in that name," that is, in the Spirit of Christ, God was not a Judge but a loving Father; "reconciliation" meant that God Himself had sent forth His Son to make men friends with Him, to end the quarrel which sin had begun; "atonement" meant, not something done to propitiate God, but a moving act of love which generated love and brought man home—"at one" with God. The Modernists see that the very meaning of salvation has largely been lost. As long as men thought of salvation as Jonathan Edwards did, as escape from an endless hell of physical torture, their souls were shaken at the thought of the fate that might be theirs. But few men now believe in "hell," and because they have become sceptical of hell, salvation has no meaning for them. Nor do they respond to the appeal once so powerful that salvation means deliverance from sin, for they identify that salvation with selfishness. What advantage would it be to be delivered from sin if that were the end? Man would simply stand in this universe without the need of God. We need to return to the fundamental thought of salvation, that it is not negative but positive; that it is not deliverance *from* something but deliverance to God.

If the popular conception of salvation in the Protestant churches be carefully examined, it will be found that it means salvation *from* God, a fearful Being. But to the saints of old it meant salvation *to* God. The psalmist expressed the deepest longings of the soul when he cried: "My soul is athirst for God, yea even for the living God. When shall I come to appear before the presence of God?" Now, it was this salvation that Jesus brought. Those who became his disciples had "boldness" to enter into the presence of God, and found Him not a hostile Power but a strong and loving Friend of the human soul—the Father who pities man's infirmities and would have him enter into communion with Him. This was the salvation that Jesus brought and the salvation which Paul preached—the salvation which Augustine expressed in golden words: "Thou hast made us for Thyself and our hearts are restless till they rest in Thee."

The Modernist would not pause at the sixteenth century. He desires to make the ancient tradition a living power to-day, to reveal the heroic spirit of the early disciples, to show that their Creeds were not the result of metaphysical speculation but were the expression of a deep spiritual experience. If the experience has expanded, then the Creeds can no longer fully express that experience; they can only partially express it. Therefore he is not dominated by the Creeds. He recognizes that they were once necessary dikes to check the tide of futile speculation. They were the expression of a phase of the Church's life, and he does not look to any dogmatic statement that might be put forth today to do the same work. It must be done by life—a life that is a witness to the world of the power of Christ. He would lead men back to the study of the New Testament, recognizing that while that represents the interpretation—and sometimes the erroneous interpretation—of the life of Jesus, it is possible through it to come into touch with Jesus Christ with such spiritual reality as will produce in their lives the effects produced by the Presence of Jesus in days gone by. He would lead men back to the study of the Old Testament, that they might see that God did not wait till man had outgrown animism, polytheism, anthropomorphism, and low moral conceptions of God and man, before He revealed Himself, but that He came to the Jews as they were and gradually lifted them from a lower plane to a higher, until they could be prepared to receive God's final revelation of Himself, when in the fulness of time He sent forth His Son. But all this is dependent upon man's conception of God.[2]

I am told that at the "Bishops' Meeting" at Carnegie Hall in November last, the Honorable John J. Davis, Secretary of Labor, made a most moving speech, in which he described the simple piety of his mother which had influenced himself and his brothers, supporting them in the hard struggle against poverty and leading them to the Christian life. But at the end, thinking no doubt that the new generation was forgetting the influence of such a life as his mother had revealed, he turned upon the Modernists and declared that they would not rest satisfied until they had "modernized God." This, I am told, was received with laughter and applause. Had it been my privilege to hear this speech, I am sure I should have joined both in the laughter and in the applause—in the laughter because it was a shrewd thrust at the Modernist, and wit is always delightful, but I should have joined in the applause perhaps for other reasons than actuated the majority, for to me it seems a fine definition of the real purpose of the Modernist, to "modernize God."

For if Mr. Davis had considered what lay back of the beautiful life of his mother, he would have been obliged to recognize that it was due to the modernization of God. Had God never been modernized, Mr. Davis and his brothers and all of us would still be digging for roots in the forests of the Old World, decked out in a fashionable garment of vermilion and blue paint! It was because Christian men came into England and finally penetrated to the mountains of Wales that the old gods of the Druids were displaced and a "modern" God reigned in their stead. The whole history of Jewish and Christian religion is the record of the modernizing of God. When Moses saw the burning bush and drew near in reverence, he heard the voice of God proclaiming Himself with a new name, a "modern" name, a name that never had been known to the patriarchs. When Solomon built his temple, God was glorified with a new name, the "Lord of Hosts." He was no longer conceived as the tribal God Who dwelt upon Mount Sinai, but as a Presence leading the host for the accomplishment of a noble purpose. When Isaiah saw the vision of the Holy One, it was a "modern" God, a God greater, nobler, purer, holier than had ever been conceived of before. But he whom we call the second Isaiah had a still more modern thought of God, revealed in the suffering Servant of Jehovah, "wounded for our transgressions," upon whom the Lord hath laid "the iniquity of us all."

Then when Jesus came, it was a "modern" God whom he declared.[3] He used the same word that the psalmist had used and called God Father, but it was with an absolutely new interpretation that he used the ancient formula. God had been conceived as a Father by the men of old, but a Father only of Israel. But Jesus reveals Him as the Father of all mankind. Indeed, it was the modernizing of God which led to the crucifixion of Jesus. Had he been content with the old conception of God, he might have lived undisturbed and talked to men about the lilies of the field and the birds of the air and the beauty of kindliness one to another. But it was because he said that God was his Father, that he was in the Father and the Father was in him, that those who saw him saw the Father, that the orthodox were led to put him to death.

Stephen was a "Modernist." It was because he believed that the old conception of God which underlay the law and the prophets was an inadequate conception and tried to lead men to the worship of the Father of our Lord Jesus Christ, that he was stoned to death. It was a "modern" God whom Paul preached throughout the cities of Asia Minor and Greece, for he was proclaiming God not alone as a Transcendent Being far removed from human life, but as Incarnate in the Man Christ Jesus, and that led men to declare that he was "turning the world upside down." Athanasius, Augustine (in certain moods), Aquinas, St. Francis, the great Reformers, all the leaders of the Church, have modernized God. But when we say they have "modernized" God, it is not meant that they have made a new God, any more than Columbus made a new continent. They have discovered more of God than had ever been known before, and that discovery has shown that some of the old conceptions of God were incompatible with the Eternal Spirit of Holiness, Goodness, Beauty, and Truth. "His Truth endureth from generation to generation," yet each new discovery of the scientist and each vital experience of the saint makes it modern.

Always these modernizations were due in part to the influence of a larger understanding of the world and a deeper appreciation of the spirit of man. In other words, the modern conception of God is as truly a revelation of God as that which was given to Moses by the voice from the burning bush. Revelation is a continuous process, because we are in communion with the living God; because man is being enriched by the larger knowledge and the wider experience of life. God, then, must be modernized in the twentieth century in such a way that men shall feel that they can draw near to Him Whose Wisdom is being revealed by the discovery of nature, by the analysis of the soul, by the intercommunion between men of different races and religious experiences. The only difference, then, between the Modernist and the Fundamentalist is that the Fundamentalist insists that the earliest revelation of God is the final one, and the Modernist is inspired by the expectation given by Jesus himself that God, who is Spirit, will more and more lead His children into the Truth.

It has been finely stated that the greatest revolution in theological thought in the eighteen centuries which have passed since the death of the last Apostle has come in our own time—in the last fifty years, in the passing from the thought of the Sovereignty of God to the Fatherhood of God. As a dogma, that has always been accepted; as a living truth, it is the discovery of the nineteenth century.* Such a revolution cannot fail to affect deeply the religious life. That theological revolution was coterminous with an intellectual revolution brought about by the discoveries of physical science, and now being consolidated by psychological investigation. Now, if the ancient formulas in their literal and original meaning be insisted upon as conditions of membership in the Church or as necessary for the exercise of the ministry, it cannot fail that while those of the clergy and laity who have adjusted the old faith to the new

* I am indebted for this thought to the Reverend Edward H. Ward, D.D., Rector of St. Luke's Church, Hot Springs, Virginia.

knowledge have been able to do this because they have absorbed the new knowledge slowly, the same result cannot be expected from the young life which has come to the new knowledge either without the old faith or in spite of it. They are asking that they may be relieved from the burden which they cannot or will not bear. No repetition of the dogma will bring relief. It will only increase scepticism.

If the purpose of the Modernist were understood, I believe that even those who find themselves unable to agree with certain conclusions which he has reached, who are troubled and perplexed because he can be no longer satisfied with the ancient clothing, would recognize that like David, though he cannot wear the armor of Saul and must fight the battle untrammelled, he may be a "man after God's own heart," and instead of reviling him as did David's brethren, would say with Saul, "Go and the Lord be with you." For the fact is that the enemy which confronts the Church to-day must be met in a new way. Every one is lamenting the weakness of the Church, its failure to do the great work that was done of old; and in this spirit of despondency, they magnify the power of the enemy and do not consider where the weakness of the Church may lie. It lies primarily, I believe, in this: that many men and women have identified the religion of Jesus with orthodoxy. Orthodoxy requires nothing but obedience. It does not stimulate the intellect. It does not stir the emotions, except the emotions of fear and hatred; and as a result, many of the people in the churches have lost all understanding of the obligation laid upon them as disciples of Jesus Christ, and men outside of the Church think that while they are saying "Lord, Lord" yet they are not doing the will of the Father; and they believe that the repetition of the formula actually prevents the will from accomplishing God's purpose.

The orthodox are very apt to lay emphasis upon the statement in the book of Acts that the disciples were of one heart and one mind. But they forget that that was but one characteristic of the primitive Brotherhood, and, in my judgment, misunderstand the unity. The "one mind" was the belief that in Jesus, the Messiah —Israel's Ideal—had been revealed; the "one heart" was loving devotion to their Lord. The words reveal "unity of Spirit in the bond of peace." There were two other characteristics: first, an intense enthusiasm for the evangelization of the world. Yet how many who "profess and call themselves Christians" feel no such obligation, but rather question whether it is desirable or possible to make the way of Christ known to mankind! And when we come to the third characteristic of the primitive Brotherhood, many refuse even to listen to it: "Neither did they call the things which they possessed their own, but had all things in common." The very reading of the text causes a well-to-do congregation to shiver: "Will it not lead to Communism, to Socialism, to Bolshevism, to anarchy?" (They do not distinguish these words; they lump them all together as if they meant the same thing, recognizing them to be the enemies of the self-satisfied possessors of property.) It is not necessary to be a Bolshevist, an anarchist, a Communist, or a Socialist. Many of the Modernists believe that Socialism is a political heresy and that it would produce the disease which it attempts to cure. But we cannot escape from the revelation of the essential obligation of Christian men not to call the things which they possess their own. They may retain the property in their hands, but if they are Christians they can retain it only as trustees. They must use their judgment in its distribution, but distribute it they must. Now because the Modernist—being a Fundamentalist—recognizes that these three things are the essentials of the Christian Church to-day, as they were in the beginning, he desires to "modernize" God in order that he may spiritualize human society.*

These three notes of the primitive community the Modernist believes to be as essential to-day as they were in the beginning. But to him the evangelization of the world does not mean carrying to the heathen the orthodoxy of the past. He believes it means preaching to them Jesus Christ, the only full and perfect revelation of God. But he recognizes that that evangelization cannot be carried on by sectarian mission-

* It is not to be supposed that the Modernist claims that he alone recognizes that these are the characteristics of true Christianity. He knows that none have been more zealous to make Christ's way known, "His saving health among all nations," than have the Fundamentalists; that the Anglo-Catholics have been among the most fearless in the proclamation of a true Christian "Communism." But he does think that the Modernist has, in addition to these two, a truer understanding of the meaning of unity than is possible to those who identify it with either the acceptance of ancient formularies or the perpetuation of a venerable form of ministry.

ary societies nor by separate churches. It needs the fellowship of all who "profess and call themselves Christians." He knows that that evangelization will be ineffective while Christian nations are at war one with another. He is convinced that the evangelization of the world must be preceded by the casting down of the idol of nationalism, in order that the ideal of brotherhood may dominate.

He, too, believes that the Church must be of one heart and of one mind, but he does not interpret that as the unity of obedience or of opinion, but as the unity of spirit, the spirit of life manifesting itself in infinite variety, united in the revelation of God's purpose for mankind.

He is not tied up to any economic or political theory, but he is convinced that for the Church to admit that degrading poverty and prostitution (the two intimately connected) are the inevitable accompaniments of civilization, is not only the condemnation of civilization but would lead to the destruction of the Church. Until the spirit of Divine Communism—which does not call for the abrogating of personal property but does demand that personal property shall be conceived as a trust, to be used not for the self-indulgence of the owner nor to lead those nearest to him into the degradation of luxury, but for the benefit of the community, that is, for the commonwealth—is recognized as the essential requirement for the Church to-day, men will continue to believe that the Christian Church is the embodiment of selfishness.[4]

The Modernist knows that there are many men and women who are interested in one or another of these essential elements of the Church, who yet are repelled by the Church, and he is seeking to reveal the glory of the Church to these men and women, that their lives may be inspired by that revelation of the Perfect Life, to which the Church exists to bear witness. He knows that unless the Church can be revivified by a blood infusion, it will die of pernicious anemia.

Now, when the motive of the Modernist is thus apprehended, it will be found that in many points, both Fundamentalist and Traditionalist are in sympathy with him. What a tragedy it would be if it should be declared that the spirit of the Modernist must be incarnated outside the Christian Church. But on the other hand, if those who represent the majority in all the churches to-day could see the signs of the times, I believe that they would no longer be insisting that the foundation of the faith rests on opinions which have doubtful historical witness, which are in conflict with man's larger knowledge of himself and of the universe in which he lives and are unworthy of the God and Father of our Lord Jesus Christ and that they would say with the Apostle: "Grace be unto you and to all who love the Lord Jesus Christ in sincerity."

The controversy in the churches has not arisen independently of other great movements in human society. It is but one indication of the "earthquake and the whirlwind and the fire" which have shaken the world. If with the prophet we could recognize that these are preliminaries to the hearing of the "still, small voice"; if with Jesus, instead of being terrified, we could lift up our hearts and recognize that the Kingdom of God is nigh at hand, how full of courage and hope and love the heart would be! As we look back over history, we see that many of the great revivals of religion have been preceded by a "renaissance," a deeper understanding of the meaning of the past, a more glowing realization of the powers of man, and grateful and humble recognition that the world can only be saved by the grace of God apprehended by faith.

The signs of the times are not altogether terrifying. The American Bible Society has issued twice the number of Bibles in the past year ever printed in any year before, so great is the demand for the Word of God. The newspapers, in spite of their startling headlines and misrepresentations, are aware of the wide-spread interest in religion. Not for centuries has there been in every gathering of men and women, whether in clubs or in private houses, such a manifestation of interest in religious problems. They are weary of the controversy about words, but they hunger and thirst after righteousness.

If only the Church could reveal the foundations, the fundamentals, I believe there would come—I believe there is at hand—such a revival of religion as will purify society, inspire the nations of the world, and bring hope to the backward nations. To some of us it seems as if the Modernist were the one who most clearly sees the signs of the times.

The purpose of this book is to allay fears by revealing the true purpose of the Modernist.

If I have succeeded, it will not be necessary for the Fundamentalist or the Traditionalist to agree with some of its conclusions. I shall be glad if some of their fears be allayed. If these fears were allayed, the Church would be in a position to consider what it would be best to do in regard to the Creeds. I have stated elsewhere[5] why I think no loss would be entailed by the frank acknowledgment that the Creeds need no longer be recited in the Service of the Church but kept—all of them—as witnesses of the eternal faith in the expressions which the men of old found satisfying; that if some creed be thought essential, though as has been pointed out the Church for four centuries felt no such necessity, then it might be well to use the formula in the Catechism which interprets the Doctrine of the Trinity in a way that makes it helpful instead of in a way that to many is puzzling. This would not be such a radical departure from tradition as it might at first seem to be. If any one will turn to the service for the Holy Communion in the American Prayer Book and look at the "Special Prefaces" he will note that the first one for Trinity Sunday is a highly theological formula, which few of the laity understand and which I think the clergy will admit it is not easy even for those who have studied the question for years to interpret. Our fathers felt this difficulty and therefore added a new Preface, which expresses most beautifully the spiritual value of the doctrine: "It is very meet, right, and our bounden duty, that we should at all times, and in all places, give thanks unto thee, O Lord, Holy Father, Almighty, Everlasting God. For the precious death and merits of thy Son Jesus Christ our Lord, and for the sending to us of the Holy Ghost, the Comforter; who are one with thee in thy Eternal Godhead."*

On the other hand, there are many Modernists, probably the majority, who strongly object to this, and would prefer that the Creeds should remain as they are and be used in the Service as they have been used for many centuries, allowing the same liberty of interpretation as the Church has always allowed. This would require no official action on the part of the Convention. All that it would require would be a change of heart. When the panic has subsided—and I believe that when the position of

* See Prayer Book, pp. 232 and 234.

the Modernist is understood, it will subside—and to speak bluntly, if some who are called Modernists do not stir up the minds of the faithful by rash or offensive utterances; if the people will cease to identify Modernism with every fad and eccentricity which they may hear of; and finally, if the men who are trying to revolutionize the Church and make it less and less Protestant, and more and more Roman, will not be looked on as representing the "faith once" for all "delivered to the Saints"; if the "saving common sense" of the bishops can make itself effective, as I believe when the panic subsides it will do; then I think there will be a prospect of the Church being able to serve God in "all Godly quietness."

Because I believe this, I look forward to a revival of religion in which the Episcopal Church will play an important part, not by attempting to absorb the other churches, but by such co-operation with them that we shall draw near to that Fellowship with God's Son which the great Apostle hoped for centuries ago, but which has never been fully realized. But this consummation is dependent upon two fundamentals which seem to have been ignored

—fundamentals laid down by Jesus himself: First, "Call no man your master upon earth for one is your master, even Christ"; second, "All ye are brethren"—therefore, "Love one another."

NOTES

PREFACE

[1] "Origin and Evolution of Religion," by E. Washburn Hopkins, Ph.D., LL.D.

"A Student's Philosophy of Religion," by William Kelley Wright, Ph.D.

"Is Christian Experience an Illusion?" by Henry Balmforth, M.A.

"Problems of Religion," by Durant Drake, M.A., Ph.D.

CHAPTER I

[1] See Hastings' "Encyclopedia of Religion and Ethics," vol. VIII, "Modernism," p. 763.

[2] See "Mystical Religion" and "Essays and Addresses on the Philosophy of Religion," by Baron Friedrich von Hügel.

[3] See "A Much Abused Letter" and "Christianity at the Cross Roads," by G. Tyrrell.

[4] See "Encyclopedia Britannica," closing paragraph of article "Roman Catholic Church," by Viscount St. Cyrs.

[5] *Op. cit. supra* (No. 1).

[6] See "Modernism and the Person of Christ," by W. J. Sparrow Simpson, p. 7.

[7] See *The Modern Churchman*, June, 1922: "The Spirit of Modernism," p. 113.

[8] See "The Golden Bough," by Sir James Frazer, part VI, p. 412.

CHAPTER II

[1] See "The Virgin Birth of Christ," by James Orr, p. 6.

[2] See "Nature, Addresses and Lectures," by Ralph Waldo Emerson, pp. 63–64.

[3] See "Essays and Addresses on the Philosophy of Religion," by Baron Friedrich von Hügel, pp. 197–198.

[4] *Op. cit.*, p. 279.

[5] See "Problems of Religion," by Durant Drake, p. 282.

[6] See "The Conflict Between Science and Theology," by Andrew D. White.

[7] *Op. cit. supra* (No. 5), pp. 284–286.

[8] See "Mechanism, Life and Personality," by J. S. Haldane, M.D.

CHAPTER III

[1] See "St. Paul," by Adolf Deissman, p. 129 (English translation).

[2] *Op. cit.*, pp. 115–116.

[3] See "Jesus of Nazara," by Theodor Keim, vol. VI, p. 280.

[4] *Op. cit.*, vol. VI, division III.

[5] See "Freedom in the Church," by Alexander V. G. Allen, p. 194.

[6] See "The Virgin Birth," by Frederic Palmer, p. 1.

[7] See "Mont St. Michel and Chartres," by Henry Adams.

[8] See "The Lord's Controversy and His People's," a sermon by George A. Gordon, D.D., January 13, 1924.

[9] See "The Ancient Creeds in Modern Life," by H. B. Swete, p. 22.

[10] See "Belief in God," by Charles Gore, D.D., p. 275.

[11] See "St. Paul's Epistle to the Galatians," by Cyril W. Emmet, M.A.

[12] *Op. cit. supra* (No. 304), vol. II, p. 45.

[13] See "Das Fortleben des Heidentums in der Altchristlichen Kirche," by Wilhelm Soltau, pp. 77–78. Also, "Vorträge und Aufsätze," by Hermann Usener, p. 163.

[14] *Boston Transcript*, January 12, 1924: "A Roman Churchman's Views on the Authenticity of the Virgin Birth."

[15] See Hebrew lexicon of Brown, Driver and Briggs.

[16] See "The Acts of the Apostles from the Codex Bezæ," by Canon J. M. Wilson, D.D.

[17] See "The Virgin Birth," a sermon preached by Maude Royden, printed in the *Christian Century* (Chicago), February 21, 1924.

[18] *Op. cit. supra* (No. 10), p. 274. (A full discussion of this matter from the Traditionalist point of view is ably stated in this book, pp. 274–282.)

CHAPTER IV

[1] See "Revolutionary New England," by James Truslow Adams, p. 56.

[2] See "A Message to the Diocese," by the Rt. Rev. William T. Manning, D.D., D.C.L., LL.D., p. 11, delivered February 3, 1924.

[3] See "The Virgin Birth," by Frederic Palmer, p. 16.

[4] *Op. cit. supra* (No. 1), p. 37.

[5] See "The Apostles' Creed," by Arthur C. McGiffert. See also "Freedom in the Church," by Alexander V. G. Allen, chap. IV.

[6] See "Jesus and the Christian Religion," by Francis A. Henry, D.D.

[7] *Cf.* "Ordo Romanus Primus," ed. by Atchley, p. 80; quoted in "Freedom in the Church," by Alexander V. G. Allen, p. 200.

[8] See "The Foundations of Belief," by the Rt. Hon. Arthur J. Balfour, part IV, chap. III.

[9] See "Life of Daniel Webster," by Henry Cabot Lodge, chap. VI.

[10] See "Freedom in the Church" (Allen), pp. 196–197.

[11] See "The Crisis of the Churches," chap. IX.

CHAPTER V

[1] See "The New Order of Sainthood," by Henry Fairfield Osborn. Also "From Immigrant to Inventor," by Michael Pupin, p. 191, and chaps. VII and XI.

[2] See "The Origin and Permanent Value of the Old Testament," by Charles Foster Kent, Ph.D.

[3] See "Christ's Thought of God," by Canon James M. Wilson.

[4] See "The Social Message of the Modern Pulpit," by Charles Reynolds Brown.

[5] See "The Crisis of the Churches."